READING WIREDU

WORLD PHILOSOPHIES

Bret W. Davis, D. A. Masolo, and Alejandro Vallega, editors

READING WIREDU

BARRY HALLEN

INDIANA UNIVERSITY PRESS

This book is a publication of

Indiana University Press
Office of Scholarly Publishing
Herman B Wells Library 350
1320 East 10th Street
Bloomington, Indiana 47405 USA

iupress.org

Cover portrait: Sketch of Kwasi Wiredu by Agyenim Wiredu, June 5, 2020.

Manufactured in the United States of America
First Printing 2021

Library of Congress Cataloging-in-Publication Data

Names: Hallen, B., author.
Title: Reading Wiredu / Barry Hallen.
Description: Bloomington, Indiana : Indiana University Press, [2021] |
    Series: World philosophies | Includes bibliographical references and
    index.
Identifiers: LCCN 2020043805 (print) | LCCN 2020043806 (ebook) | ISBN
    9780253057020 (hardback) | ISBN 9780253057013 (paperback) | ISBN
    9780253057006 (ebook)
Subjects: LCSH: Wiredu, Kwasi. | Philosophy, African—20th century.
Classification: LCC B5619.G433 W574 2021 (print) | LCC B5619.G433 (ebook)
    | DDC 199/.667—dc23
LC record available at https://lccn.loc.gov/2020043805
LC ebook record available at https://lccn.loc.gov/2020043806

à la famiglia: charles spurgeon · reginald · olga · joyce ·
jerry · carla · florence · george · betty lou ("sis") · barbara ·
jean · john jr. · john ("pac") · lilian · mary katherine ·
melvina ("mel") · paul melvin ("pauli") · paul murphy ·
("tang") · robert cowan · robert e. · stephanie elizabeth ·
paula · nellie ("nell") · jason · russell · darien · alex ·
paulette ("sandy") · fannie ("dood") · lizzie ("ti") · murphy
("murph") · cassandra michelle · cliff · elizabeth grace ·
isaac michael · nora faye · scott · terri · nora

CONTENTS

READING WIREDU

Introduction

THIS LITTLE BOOK IS MEANT to serve as an introduction to the thought of the philosopher Kwasi Wiredu. Some colleagues may say he needs no introduction because he has been recognized as one of the most important philosophers of Africa for many years. There are two problems with that sentiment. I speak for myself, as his colleague and friend, when I say that for too many years I failed to understand his overall approach to philosophy. That changed when I undertook the comprehensive review of his work that the writing of this text required.

Second, Wiredu the philosopher never meant for his work to be confined to the subdiscipline of African philosophy. Citizen of Ghana and graduate of Oxford University, Wiredu has been typed as an analytic philosopher. Yet in this book, he will say, "I am *not* an analytic philosopher." His adoption of what he describes as a "genetic methodology" is certainly a radical departure from the analytic tradition. He uses it to explore environmental considerations that have given rise to various forms of thought. His criticisms of American philosopher W. V. O. Quine and reflections thereon are based in part on applications of it.

Understandably, in professional circles, some may ask how the genetic dimension to Wiredu's philosophy could have gone under-reported for so long. Perhaps in part because Wiredu writes relatively short, focused, and tightly argued essays. His two published books are edited collections of those essays. There is no book by him that provides a synoptic, comprehensive overview of his thought. To arrive at the one represented by this text, I've had to interrelate any number of his writings.

Wiredu does commit to the defense of African philosophy—to philosophy as an intellectual exercise that had, has, and deserves a place in Africa's indigenous cultural heritage. He does so as an academician and draws upon his native Akan culture to demonstrate that African languages and cultures are as valuable resources for philosophy as are Western languages and cultures. However, throughout he also maintains a transcendent intellectual posture that enables him, given his cross-cultural background, to undertake original analyses of academic philosophy itself. Consequently, Wiredu is much more than an African philosopher who does African philosophy. He has important things to say about academic philosophy generally—regarding the philosophy of language, ontology, epistemology, ethics, and social and political philosophy.

My hope is that those who take the time to digest the contents of this little book will be persuaded to think of him in those terms. His original ways of doing philosophy and the ideas that result have long deserved more attention than they are receiving.

ONE

On Quine, Logic, and Ontology

BEGINNING IN 1973, KWASI WIREDU[1] published a series of four articles in the journal *Second Order: An African Journal of Philosophy*. All were entitled "Logic and Ontology" and all focused critically, in part, on the work of the American philosopher W. V. O. Quine. Quine had become interested in the legendary *problem of universals*. Briefly, that problem first arose thousands of years ago over issues relating to the nature of *existence* generally and to whether abstract ideas (e.g., mathematics) are merely transient human inventions or discoveries about the nature of reality. Quine proposed a thesis intended to redefine and restrict the meaning of "existence." His definition was meant to allow targeted contents of systematic theories to be treated as actually describing the world while avoiding the apparently insoluble problems involved in formulating an all-encompassing theory of existence.

Since the time of Plato and his realm of the forms, philosophers have been trying to resolve what is known as the problem of universals.[2] The word "particulars" can be used to refer to the multitude of material objects that are said to exist in the world. "Universals," on

---

1. Pronounced *Kwa*-(soft *a* as in English-language "father")-*see Weer*-(as in English-language "beer")-*ree-due*.

2. For those unfamiliar with Plato on this, he maintains that the paradigm of every imaginable kind of thing (universals)—dog, tree, beauty, number,

the other hand, seem very different from those particulars. The standard catalog of universals can include numbers (mathematics, etc.), qualities (redness), attributes (patience), properties (wisdom), classes (people who are handicapped, fans of Liverpool FC), and relations (between, next, after, before). Universals come into play when human beings begin to understand, talk about, and manipulate particulars. Sometimes human beings talk about universals without any reference to particulars (the meaning of the concept "good").

The problem of universals involves determining the existential status, the nature of the existence, of these abstractions. It may therefore also be viewed as a problem of ontology.[3] Are universals or abstractions as real as the so-called particular material objects, in the sense that they also exist independently of the human beings who use them? Think of the way we use mathematics to facilitate space exploration. Is that because mathematics is somehow built into the structure of the universe, latent there until human beings uncover and involve it in their interstellar explorations? Or is mathematics an original human invention, a kind of tool that is useful for all kinds of things but would disappear from the universe altogether with the extinction of humankind and its invented abstract ideas?

The philosopher W. V. O. Quine, who will feature prominently in what follows, has produced a helpful summary of the irreconcilable positions academic philosophers take on the existential status of universals.

realism (Plato et al.):
> universals or abstract entities have being independently of the mind; the mind may discover them but it cannot create them. (Quine 1980, 14)

conceptualism (Ockham, Descartes, Locke, Hume):
> there are universals and they are mind-made. (Quine 1980, 14)

---

triangle, etc.—that ordinary objects in the world imitate exists in a separate realm accessible only to and by a properly conditioned intellect.

3. Ontology is the subdiscipline of philosophy concerned with what exists and the nature of existence.

on the basis of our experience of the world of particulars our
minds can invent concepts (redness) that can then relate to more
general elements of those particulars (Grayling 1998, 211–12).

nominalism/formalism (Hobbes, Carnap):
there are no such things as *existent* abstract entities, including
those which are said to be mind-made; there are only
particulars. . . . the various abstract entities (mathematics) which
human beings mistakenly come to believe are real are nothing
more than invented notations that sometimes serve as tools
which can be helpful in performing certain operations but have
no linguistic significance (reference) to things that are real.
(paraphrased from Quine 1980, 14–15)

After millennia of controversy, academic philosophers have yet to arrive at a consensus about which of these alternatives is to be preferred.
The problem of universals, therefore, is still very much of a problem.

Controversy arose anew when Quine proposed an *existential thesis*
that he thought would avoid the confusions that led to the problem
of universals becoming a problem. For one thing, Quine finds philosophers' reliance upon *ordinary language* to express their ideas an
important source of the confusion. *Ordinary* language means how
the words of a language are used by people in everyday life. In such
circumstances, people do not go to great lengths to define their terminology explicitly, so how a word or expression is *used* in effect becomes
its meaning. Ordinary language can therefore be vague and impre-
cise and give rise to misunderstandings when involved with technical
philosophical issues. According to Quine, this is a fault that affects
many of the texts that have been promoted over the centuries as solutions to the problem of universals. "By showing how to circumvent the
problematic parts of ordinary usage . . . we show the problems to be
purely verbal" (Quine 1960, 261).

One of Quine's favorite examples of how ordinary language involving "existence" can confound rational thinking relates to the existential status of the mythical horse Pegasus. As mythical, Pegasus cannot
exist because myths are made-up stories rather than statements of
historical fact. Yet there have been philosophers who have said that

because we continue to talk about Pegasus, he must exist. This view can give rise to the following conundrums: "If Pegasus *were* not . . . we should not be talking about anything when we use the word, therefore it would be nonsense to say even that Pegasus is not. [Therefore] Pegasus is" (Quine 1980, 2). And: "The old notion that Pegasus cannot be said not to be without presupposing that in some sense Pegasus is" (1980, 8). Quine puts part of the blame on "philosophers who have united in ruining the good old word 'exist'" (1980, 3), something he wants to put right.

Quine's alternative is to propose a *thesis that provides a simple and therefore clear form of expression* that can be used to assert that something *exists*. He thinks his existential thesis will provide relief from the established but irreconcilable theories previously outlined, as well as a more focused and less controversial but still philosophically astute sense of existence.[4] Because ordinary language is not up to the task, Quine needs to find a more technically precise medium to use for the expression and application of the thesis. His medium of choice turns out to be *formal logic*.

According to Quine, over the course of its history, humanity has constructed all sorts of theories about the world that involve both *physical objects* and *classes*.[5] What he means by physical *objects* should be obvious. "Class" is Quine's term for *abstractions*, which he refuses to call *universals* thanks to Plato and therefore describes as *abstract objects*. If our theories about the world are to make any sense, we need to be able to say these things exist. "Let us keep in mind also that knowledge normally develops in a multiplicity of theories, each with its limited utility and each, unless it harbors more danger than utility, with its internal consistency" (Quine 1960, 251).

Reflection on the contents of theories is enough to justify the observation that they contain lots of abstract entities (now linked to

---

4. "Quine's criterion of ontological commitment has dominated ontological discussion in analytic philosophy since the middle of the 20th century; it deserves to be called the orthodox view" (Bricker 2016).

5. In what follows, whenever Quine uses the term *object* or *objects*, it will be highlighted in italics. I am doing this because his sustained use of this English-language term will be central to Wiredu's critique.

classes). "I have appealed to *classes* and recognized them as *abstract objects*" (Quine 1960, 243n5).[6] Presumably these classes contain the varieties of *universals* previously listed: numbers, properties, attributes, relations, and so forth (Quine 1960, 233–76).[7] For example, the class of numbers will contain the class of even numbers, the class of qualities will contain the class of colors (red, blue, green, etc.), and so forth.

The word "class," which Quine uses as a synonym for "abstractions," can be regarded as a more technical substitute for ordinary language's "group," "type," or "kind." Classes can qualify as *objects* because Quine treats them as real. In the present context, "real" means that when treated as components of theories, they are said to exist. Classes may also be composed of other classes. The class of red things could be contained by the more general class of (all) colored *objects*—red, blue, green, and so forth.

This is important because we are being introduced to Quine's own very carefully constructed response to the problem of universals. To begin, Quine refuses to use the word "universals" because it is so strongly identified with Plato and his realm of the forms. He prefers to speak of classes, which exist and contain the abstractions that qualify as real. We need them to be real if our theories about the world are to make sense.

Quine refuses to go further than this—to elaborate a more conventionally philosophical analysis of a general notion of *existence*—because that would resurrect the old irreconcilable controversies relating to the problem of universals. "The abstract *objects* that it is useful to admit to the universe of discourse at all seem to be adequately explicable in terms of a universe comprising just *physical objects* and all *classes* of the *objects* in the universe (hence classes of physical *objects*, *classes* of such *classes* [higher abstractions], etc.). At any rate I think of no persuasive exceptions" (Quine 1960, 267; my emphasis).

---

6. "Quine assumes that the real numbers are objects existing antecedently to mathematical thought" (Wiredu 1973b, 36).

7. "Red *things* . . . all belong to the *class* of red things. . . . Ordinary *objects of any kind* can be members of *classes*: as well as the *class* of red things, there is the *class* consisting of everything larger than me" (Grayling 1998, 211; my emphasis).

Common sense could possibly qualify as a kind of overall practical theory or mélange of such theories that involve physical *objects* and innumerable *classes*.[8] But the kinds of theories Quine thinks philosophers should prioritize are those propounded by the disciplines whose avowed interest is knowledge arising from a disciplined methodology: the natural or "hard" sciences as well as "softer" scientific disciplines such as psychology, economics, sociology, and history (Quine 1995, 49). To repeat, it makes good sense that for the theories of such disciplines to be significant, the *objects* (physical and abstract) to which they make reference must exist.

According to Quine, the issue of what exists is best approached on the basis of what a theory says there is rather than by philosophers undertaking some sort of independent empirical research to confirm or deny claims made by the theory (Quine 1960, 243n5). This is an important point. Philosophers are not scientists who are mandated to do firsthand experimentation about what exists in, for example, the natural world. But they are entitled to concern themselves with the knowledge claims of theories—what theories say exists—formulated by scientists who do study that world.

Quine has said he needs a *more precise medium than ordinary language* to express theoretical existence. He finds that linguistic precision by using the notation, the symbolization, of *formal or propositional logic*. By preferring the severity of logical notation, he stays as far away as possible from the existential confusions of ordinary language and other philosophers.

I can empathize with the possibly mixed responses of those who are reading this and becoming concerned that they may not be able to follow his argument because they do not have a background in formal logic. That can be remedied by using a bit of extraordinary language coupled with somewhat intuitive insights into the solutions he proposes. Bear in mind that Quine thinks he is simplifying things by dealing with existence as limited to claims made by theories. Once

---

8. "Theory may be deliberate, as in a chapter on chemistry, or it may be second nature, as in the immemorial doctrine of ordinary enduring middle-sized physical objects" (Quine 1960, 11).

again, his aim is to avoid the confusions arising from the innumerable texts addressing the problem of universals that have not succeeded, in part, because of confusions arising from their reliance upon ordinary language.

Quine's introductory logical formulations of his thesis are relatively simple. Here are those formulations and supplementary explanations of their logical components as elements of the *formal language* he recommends as sufficient for expressing theoretical statements involving the existence of physical *objects* and *classes* or abstract *objects*.[9]

(1) $[(x) \, Gx]$ = a template, form, or pattern to be used for the expression of *general* theoretical statements

or

(2) $[(\exists x) \, Gx]$ = a template, form, or pattern to be used for the expression of *particular* theoretical statements.

This is *formal* logic, so (1) and (2) should be regarded as forms that can be filled with whatever content constitutes the theory. These are forms or templates in the same sense as the symbolic expression "$2 + 2 = 4$" is a form or template. To be applied, it needs to be filled with specific content about whatever is being counted—for example, 2 bicycles + 2 bicycles = 4 bicycles.

The first symbols that occur in (1) and (2)—(x) and $(\exists x)$, respectively—represent the *number* of particular or abstract *objects* (classes) mentioned by a theoretical statement. These logical symbols are therefore known as *quantifiers*. The (x) at the beginning of (1) is known as the *universal quantifier* because it is used for giving symbolic representation to the part of a theoretical statement that talks about a large number of *objects*, such as "Every ? is such that (the question mark stands for the type of *object*, yet to be specified) ..." The $(\exists x)$ at the beginning of (2) is known as the *existential quantifier* because it is used for giving symbolic representation to the part of a theoretical statement that talks about at least one *object*, such as "There is an ? such that ..."

---

9. Quine's terminology and definitions of the components—quantifiers, variables, and predicates—are conventional to formal logic. What is not conventional is his use of them to assert existence in the "real" world.

Quine writes, "Such is simply the intended sense of the *quantifiers* '(x)' and '(∃x)': 'every *object x* is such that', 'there is an *object x* such that'. The *quantifiers* are encapsulations of these specially selected, unequivocally referential idioms of *ordinary language*" (1960, 242; my emphasis). He cautions us against going beyond these basic forms of quantification to elaborate the meaning of existence: "To try to elucidate the meaning of 'exists' beyond saying that 'existence is what the *existential quantifier* expresses' would be a hopeless enterprise ... [and] explication [in turn] of the existential quantifier itself, 'there is', 'there are', *explication of general existence, is a forlorn cause* (Quine 1969b, 5; my emphasis). Note that Quine is not concerned here with symbolizing arguments that contain multiple statements. The emphasis is on symbolizing individual statements that are components of theories.

The letters or symbols that constitute the rest of templates (1) and (2), the Gx, are used to represent the specific kinds of objects that theories talk about. The x half of the Gx is called a *variable*. This is because their sense can *vary* depending upon the kinds of objects the theory discusses. Let's say we have a theory that makes statements about universes generally—"Every universe is such that," which would translate as $[(x) \; ?u]$. Or a theory that refers to one specific universe and says, "There is a universe such that," which would translate as $[(∃x) \; ?u]$. The question marks stand for the letter G in the template because it has yet to be filled with theoretical content: "*Variables* and *quantification* should be used to express *what a theory says that there is*" (Quine 1960, 243n5; my emphasis). "[This] resolves questions of scope vividly and unambiguously" (Quine 1976a, 45).

The capital letter, the G half of the Gx, is called a *predicate symbol* and is used to represent the *properties* that are being attributed to the *variables* that symbolically represent the *objects* of a theory. Let's say we are dealing with a theory that wants to attribute the property *infinity* to the variable *universe*: "Every universe is infinite," which would translate as $[(x) \; Iu]$. Or with respect to one universe, "There is a universe such that it is infinite," which would translate as $[(∃x) \; Iu]$.

Finally, variables are said to be *bound* (controlled) by the *quantifiers*—the (x) or $(∃x)$ at the beginning of each expression. This is important because it is the quantifiers, when joined with the variables and predicates, that govern and assert the existence of whatever theoretical *objects* are involved.

If symbolic substitutions have been made for all of the components of a theoretical statement, they can always be translated back into words. The important point is that in this simpler form, ordinary language is avoided, and no further claims are made or can be inferred about the nature of existence generally. As Quine sums up the entire process,

> In our canonical notation of *quantification* [the x and the $\exists x$],
> then, we find the restoration of law and order [by avoiding the
> imprecisions of ordinary language, etc.]. Insofar as we adhere to this
> notation, the *objects* we are to be understood to admit are precisely
> the *objects* which we reckon to the universe of values over which the
> *bound variables of quantification* are to be considered to range. Such
> is simply the intended sense of the quantifiers '(x)' and '$(\exists x)$': every
> *object x* is such that', 'there is an *object x* such that'. The *quantifiers are
> encapsulations* of these specially selected, unequivocally referential
> idioms of *ordinary language*. To paraphrase a sentence into the
> canonical notation of quantification is, first and foremost, *to make
> its ontic* [ontology as an adjective; see footnote 3 from this chapter]
> *content explicit*, quantification being a device for talking in general of
> *objects*. (Quine 1960, 242; my emphasis)

If you find yourself wondering why so much time and effort is spent on an exercise that seems to complicate things rather than making them simple and clear, the existential status of the abstractions used by human beings all the time to understand the world and themselves does matter. We want to be reassured that our theories, arising from the perception of things and abstractions therefrom, involve the real world. Abstractions, such as "universe," are the most important and controversial components of theories. As theoretical components, they must be said to exist if the theories we formulate to understand the world and ourselves are to be treated as significant and in principle true. Let's refer to Quine's own words: "A theory is committed to [the *existence* of] those and only those entities to which the *bound* [quantification] *variables* [*objects*] of the *theory* must be capable of referring in order that the affirmations made in the *theory* be *true*" (1980, 13–14; my emphasis).

What finally is Quine saying about the *problem of universals*? He warns us that taking on the more general problem of universals involves issues that cannot be resolved. But there is an alternative. Rather than existence generally, one can be more strategic and focus on some of the more specific things philosophers should care about the most when existence is concerned. There are things that we need to exist so our theories about the world can qualify as true, such as physical objects and the abstractions that help us understand that world and ourselves. Using formal logic, their existence can be asserted in a clear and precise manner that avoids existential confusion. As Quine puts it somewhat famously, "*To be is to be the value* [*object* represented] *of a variable*" (1976b, 199).

Wiredu will disagree with Quine on both formal *philosophical* and *linguistic* grounds. To begin with, he challenges Quine's decision to use *formal logic* to express *ontological* claims—claims about the *existence of objects* in the world. He will argue that Quine cannot ignore the restrictions the discipline of philosophy places upon formal logic—about what it can and cannot be used for. Formal logic is meant to apply to *arguments* and their component *statements*. Logical expressions in this context are the results of translations into logical symbols of *statements* that were in words.

As we've seen, for example, $[(\exists x)\ Iu]$ can serve as a translation of "There is a universe such that it is infinite." *But formal logic is not to be regarded as something that can be used to refer to a real universe that exists in the real world.* Formal logic is meant to be used to analyze the *language* we use to express our *reasoning* about that world. Doing this can involve the *relationships between the concepts* we use when reasoning. In the example Quine uses, what formal logic can do is tell us how the *concept* "infinite" *relates* to the *concept* "universe." "The sole function of quantification [the 'Every' or 'There is a' in the examples about the universe] is to indicate whether a *predicate* [the *concept* "infinite"] is to be taken in the total extent of its applicability (universal quantification) [the *concept* as involving *all* universes] or only partially (existential quantification) [the *concept* as involving only that one 'universe'].

In neither case is there any necessary *reference* to *objects* (Wiredu 1973a, 74; my emphasis).

Wiredu chose "Logic and Ontology" as the title for the *Second Order* articles because he wanted to highlight his disagreements with Quine about the ways in which Quine relates these two subdisciplines. He absolutely cannot agree with what Quine says in the following passage: "To paraphrase a sentence into the canonical notation of quantification is, first and foremost, to make its ontic ['ontological' as an adjective] content explicit, quantification being a device for talking in general of *objects*" (1960, 242; my emphasis).[10]

According to Wiredu, formal logic should remain formal, focusing on *the relationships stipulated between concepts* in the contexts of statements or arguments. That way it remains an invaluable tool for exploring such *linguistic relationships* as well as for assessing the validity of the arguments of which statements are components. It most definitely should not be employed to attribute ontological or metaphysical content to the world. That should remain a concern of "metaphysics or natural science or commonsense" (Wiredu 1973a, 75).

Wiredu also disagrees with Quine's exclusive use of the word "object" for all the things that can be said to exist by theories. "Why should it be assumed that in using the 'unequivocally referential idioms of ordinary language' we are always referring to *objects*? Just to raise this question is to be stared in the face by the fact that we do in ordinary idiomatic language refer to all sorts of *things other than objects*. Don't we refer to such things as bright possibilities, lost causes, happy

---

10. Following Quine, the point has been raised that because $\exists x$ is called the existential quantifier, logicians meant for it to be used for asserting the existence of things. But someone like Wiredu, who insists on the strictly formal nature of symbolic logic, would say it is only meant to be used for the analysis of *statements asserting the existence* of something and never as a vehicle to assert *what really exists* in the world. "In as much as the name 'existential quantifier' has tended to foster the misapprehension that the logical constant it names *primarily* expresses existence, it may perhaps be a good idea to replace it with the label 'particular quantifier'" (Wiredu 1973b, 30).

dreams and so on?[11] Is it not idiomatic to say such a thing as 'There are more *possibilities* in the situation than you have taken account of'" (Wiredu 1973a, 75; my emphasis)?

In his published writings, Quine does, at one point at least, discuss alternative ontologies and the point of privileging *objects* as essential to theoretical discourse:

> Shift of language ordinarily involves a shift of ontology. There is one important sense, however, in which *the ontological question transcends linguistic convention*: How economical an ontology can we achieve and still have a language adequate to all purposes of science? In this form the question of the ontological presuppositions of science survives.
>
> For this entire language [the symbolic one he is proposing via his existential thesis] the *only ontology required*—the only range of values for the variables of quantification—consists of *concrete individuals* of some sort or other [physical objects], plus all *classes* of such entities [abstract objects], plus all classes formed from the thus supplemented totality of entities, and so on [higher abstractions of abstractions, etc.]. (1976b, 201; my emphasis)

As one of the most important and successful undertakings of human-kind, Quine prioritizes the proper expression of scientific theories. But this does not lessen the point of Wiredu's criticism and further observation that when ontological or metaphysical claims become in-volved, all sorts of logical notations can be controversial. A resolute empiricist might object (pun unintended!) to a spiritualist's use of the word "witches" as an object that has ontological legitimacy. For many people, witches are a fantasy and do not really exist.[12] If logic is kept as a purely formal discipline, as concerned exclusively with the form of statements rather than with their content, such ontological complica-tions will not arise: "It would be clear in a case like this that the quest

---

11. See Quine (1960, 245); also Wiredu (1973a, 79).

12. At one point, Quine suggests that "this is only a manner of speaking.... so we rate the statements as fake names, and the alleged propositions as fictions" (1976b, 200). Nonetheless, everything acceptable to his ontology has to be some sort of object.

for *logical form* is being bedeviled with *metaphysical* controversy. . . . Questions regarding the communicative meaningfulness [which can involve whether the things being discussed really exist] of sentences do not belong to the province of logic. They belong to semantics or to metaphysics or to some other discipline" (Wiredu 1973a, 76–77; my emphasis).

That is why logicians have no problem working with arguments composed of patently nonsensical statements. Wiredu refers to Russell's famously absurd argument that can nevertheless be given a pass for its *validity*: "If quadruplicity drinks procrastination and this stone is thinking about Vienna then quadruplicity drinks procrastination. If quadruplicity drinks procrastination, then there is something which drinks procrastination" (Wiredu 1973a, 77). The statements of which this argument is composed are certainly not empirical truths. But given its form, the argument as a whole can be a logical truth because its form satisfies what is required for an argument to be *valid*: if the premises were true, the conclusion would follow.

The critical issue, about which Wiredu says Quine remains silent, is, "What is meant by saying something *is* an *object*?" (Wiredu 1973a, 79). Wiredu rephrases the question as, "Why should '*a* is something' be invariably construed as '*a* is an *object*'" (1973a, 80)? As far as Wiredu is concerned, "Quine has never yet volunteered an explicit theory on this subject" (1973a, 79). "In Quine's *objectual* interpretation of quantifiers, there is already implicit a major thesis about *the meaning of existence*, namely, *to be is to be an object*" (1973a, 80; my emphasis). The *meaning* of "existence"—precisely what Quine has said he wanted to avoid. Despite Quine's claims not to become involved with the historical controversies surrounding the problem of universals, Wiredu argues that this is what happens. Quine's thesis is undermined by the indeterminate ontological status of the things he does endorse. By means of his existential thesis that is meant to function as a criterion of existence, Quine in effect introduces a "criterion of objecthood" (Wiredu 1973a, 79).[13]

---

13. It is relevant to bear in mind that the title of one of Quine's best-known books is *Word and Object* (1960).

This concludes the discussion of Wiredu's critique of Quine on the basis of his use of formal logic. There is additional argumentation in the four "Logic and Ontology" articles involving more technical issues relating to the philosophy of logic. The arguments selected for representation here involve methodological considerations and therefore serve as a bridge to chapter 2. In chapter 2, Wiredu will introduce a new kind of philosophical methodology that he describes as a *genetic approach* to philosophy. He will use it to argue that Quine's reliance upon objects may arise, perhaps unconsciously, from his use of the English language rather than philosophical insight.

———~/w~———

On Quine and Language

WIREDU'S EARLIEST CRITIQUE INVOLVING QUINE also appeared in the journal *Second Order*, but a year before the first of the "Logic and Ontology" articles. This criticism, which may at first seem far removed from the subject matter of chapter 1, occurs in an article entitled "On an African Orientation in Philosophy." At one point in that text, Wiredu asks, If a philosopher's thinking is fundamentally *structured by*, as well as expressed in, his native *natural language* (English, Chinese, Swahili, etc.), can it be defended as universally true on objective grounds?

How a critique that would involve Quine and natural languages generally came to be part of an article concerned with an African orientation in academic philosophy itself warrants commentary. At the time, evidence was being put forward (principally by Western academia) to make the case that there was little resembling philosophical thought in the indigenous cultures of Africa. African cultures' systems of beliefs ("belief" was a code word used in place of "knowledge"), presumably those of the more than eight hundred language-cultures of sub-Saharan Africa, were said to have been created in the absence of significant objective standards. These systems of beliefs were said to attach so much importance to preserving objectively untrue but *emotionally* satisfying traditions inherited from the past that, in intellectual terms, there was minimal incentive to develop the intellectual skills associated with critical reasoning and therefore anything comparable to philosophy.

Wiredu began the formal study of philosophy in 1952 at the University College of the Gold Coast in the British West African colony that was to become an independent Ghana. English was the language of instruction, and the curriculum was devoted almost exclusively to Western philosophy. Students' native Twi language was for use outside of that specialized educational environment.[1] Thereafter he went to Oxford University for his graduate studies. The philosophy department at Oxford University was justly famous for analytic philosophy— ordinary language philosophy and the philosophy of language generally.[2] Wiredu's thesis, supervised by Gilbert Ryle, was entitled "Knowledge, Truth and Reason."

In an intellectual environment where *language* had become an object of intense *analysis* by talented academic philosophers, Wiredu would have been an exceptional resource. He was multilingual, of course, but more important, the languages in which he enjoyed fluency, English and Twi, had not been subjected to comparative analysis by analytic philosophers. He was therefore to find himself in a privileged position to explore the differences between these two potentially very different natural languages and to project whatever consequences this might have for abstract thinking and academic philosophy generally.

Wiredu would eventually leave the UK and return to Ghana as lecturer in philosophy at the University of Ghana, Legon. Faced with the aforementioned intellectually demeaning characterizations of the "traditional" African intellect, he began to challenge these narratives as untrue and pejorative. He argued that the so-called evidence in support of them was itself the product of misunderstandings. Furthermore, he argued that anthropology was exceeding its disciplinary limits if it assumed a proprietary right to define rationality in the

---

1. Pronounced "Tvi."

2. Wiredu writes, "The teachers with whom I studied on a one-on-one basis: Gilbert Ryle, my thesis supervisor, Peter Strawson, my college tutor, and Stuart Hampshire, my special tutor were wonderful teachers and solid thinkers" (Wiredu 2002b, 329–30).

African cultural context.[3] *Rationality*, as both concept and capacity, constitutes the core of philosophy as a discipline, and it certainly was not the case that most anthropological fieldworkers were philosophically astute. In a sense, then, Wiredu and African philosophers generally were reclaiming their own territory when, by both word and deed, they reasserted the prerogative of their discipline to define the *rational* in the indigenous African context.[4]

Wiredu intended that one consequence of this reassessment of Africa's intellectual heritage would be that the subcontinent no longer occupied a space in the philosophical marketplace that was reserved for cultures that were labeled intellectually inferior. African cultures might have their intellectual issues, as did Western cultures, but they had to be approached as if engaging with the world on the basis of a shared rationality and a common intellectual integrity. This meant that the cultures of Africa and the rest of the world would now, intellectually, be on the same level playing field, another theme of the "On an African Orientation in Philosophy" essay.

Wiredu is, in effect, *re*introducing Africa to Western scholarship while also making the fairly radical claim that *any culture's natural language may predispose philosophers who are products of it to privilege certain forms of abstract thinking and understanding.* This kind of privileging had been done to Africa repeatedly, but in a negative sense when its forms of understanding were said to diverge from so-called Western

---

3. Most memorably in "How Not to Compare African Thought with Western Thought" (1980b).

4. "I believe that there is a type of African culture, and that this type is essentialist in inspiration.... African society is in type rationalistic" (Abraham 1962, 42). "The birth of the debate on African philosophy.... At the center of this debate is the concept of reason" (Masolo 1994, 1). "For Mudimbe, then, the most important questions in the debate on African philosophy are those about the epistemological groundings which define African rationality" (Masolo 1994, 182). "Many philosophers in the African context felt that religious studies and anthropology were exceeding their disciplinary limits if and when they claimed the right to define 'rationality' in the African cultural context" (Hallen 2009, 30).

paradigms.[5] Wiredu is now suggesting that something similar can be done to those Western paradigms by demonstrating they too can be less than objective. What is quite remarkable is that his first candidate for this kind of bias is one of contemporary Western philosophy's most distinguished figures, the American philosopher W. V. O. Quine.

Overall there are two *methodological* dimensions to Wiredu's philosophy. One involves *analysis*, in the same sense in which academic philosophy overall uses the term. Wiredu defines it as follows: "Philosophical analysis elucidates thought and discourse by breaking down *concepts* into their constituent *parts* and also exhibiting their *relations* with associated concepts. It also studies various *structures of language* and *the manner in which linguistic elements gain connection with extra-linguistic reality*. These are important employments for the philosophical intellect" (Wiredu 2002b, 331; my emphasis). In part, this is the viewpoint he employs in chapter 1 when he objects to Quine's misuse of formal logic and misplaced affection for objects. But it would be a mistake to type Wiredu as simply an analytic thinker.[6]

What is most distinctive about his overall methodology is that he pairs analysis with what he describes as a *genetic* approach to philosophy. "I am *not* an analytic philosopher, for, as just indicated, I believe that analysis is only one of the missions of philosophy. That there is, in addition to the analytic method, also a *genetic method* of great importance. I explained [that] long ago in *Philosophy and an African Culture* [1980d]. *Somehow some observers have not yet got round to taking seriously that passage and, indeed, other genetical reflections in my*

---

5. Representative of social anthropology: "It is not just a matter of 'seeing the other fellow's [i.e. Africans'] point of view', essential though that is. The problem is the very much more difficult one of comprehending the *unacknowledged* and *unanalysed* standpoints from which his views are taken" (Beattie 1966, 76; my emphasis). Representative of philosophy: "Observing, for example, that there exists no word for a certain concept in a language, it has sometimes been hastily concluded that the concept does not exist in it. African languages have not infrequently been subjected to such a hasty approach and not only at the hands of aliens" (Wiredu 1996d, 82).

6. "Analytic philosophy is the philosophy that regards analysis as the *entire mission* of philosophy" (Wiredu 2002b, 332; my emphasis).

publications" (2002b, 332; my emphasis). He acknowledges that "the genetic method in philosophy is as yet undeveloped" (1980c, 165). He credits the American pragmatist, John Dewey (1902, 108–15), with arousing his interest in it as a way of doing philosophy. If, as Wiredu complains, it has been underappreciated as a key *methodological* component of his own thought from very early on, it will be important here to be as clear as possible about what it involves and to identify examples of it that occur in Wiredu's published work.

According to Wiredu, a *genetic* approach aims to identify the *origins* of foundational components of human understanding. Paraphrasing John Dewey, Wiredu puts it this way: viewing "the *fundamental* features of our conceptual framework as a cumulation of developments arising out of *the needs of life in its 'transactions' with the environment*" (1980c, 170; my emphasis). As far as genetic philosophy is concerned, how human beings unconsciously or consciously cope with that environment is indispensable to understanding human understanding.

Part of the reason the genetic dimension to his thought has gone underappreciated may be that it was mistaken for a form of linguistic analysis. What sort of access to our conceptual networks does he have in mind as fundamental? In "The Biological Foundation of Universal Norms" (Wiredu 1996o), he provides an elementary example of the genetic method when he considers the origins of the *law of contradiction*. The law may be paraphrased as "a statement cannot be both true and false at the same time." Wiredu considers it to be one of "the supreme laws of thought," and refusing to observe it "would be devastating to human society" (1996o, 38). He further states, "There would be no telling when a message is affirmed or denied, and the possibility of communication would be out of the question. Worse, individual *human survival* would be in jeopardy, for if I cannot tell affirmation from denial in communication, neither can I tell the difference between my believing and not believing something. In other words, *my powers of thought,* and with it my continued membership in the club of humans, *would be at an end*" (1996o, 38; my emphasis).

Honoring the law of noncontradiction is not just a commitment to being *rational*. It is a commitment to *survival*. This means that a genetic approach can reveal "a level of [human] life *far below the level of conscious thought and cognition*" (1980c, 170; my emphasis).[7] "This immediately earmarks the requisite minimum of actual compliance [to noncontradiction] as a naturally selected factor in our equipment for survival as a species, a selection too crucial evolutionally to have been left to the tender inconsistencies of the individual psyche" (1996o, 38). This biological consideration, explained on the basis of empirical consequences, would apparently represent the critical step of a genetic account in that it "relates . . . to the very possibility of validation" (1980c, 170).[8] In the absence of the law of contradiction, it would not be possible to verify any assertion or argument.

Is this kind of argumentation and evidence sufficient to justify a *biological* approach? He compares the evidential problems of a genetic method to those complicating Kant's transcendental deduction of the categories.

> Dewey's *genetic* account of the most fundamental *canons* [how to proceed] of inquiry. For Dewey those canons emerge as *patterns in our interactions with the environment* and are only the more complex instances of tendencies that are perceivable in more elementary life forms. . . . This kind of consideration illustrates what may appropriately be called the *genetic method in philosophy*. It is, by the way, the exact antithesis of the transcendental method, (which I reject). Both methods are *distinct from the analytic method in philosophy*. (2002b, 331; my emphasis)

Kant has to infer the categories on the basis of examples of human understanding.[9] Wiredu's genetic approach will "seek to go beyond, more specifically *below*, the level of full-blown human experience. But, in as much as every *level of life* appealed to is open to empirical examination" (1980c, 164–65), any analogy with the comparatively

---

7. For the surrounding context, see Wiredu (1980c, 165–71).

8. He praises David Hume for anticipating the genetic approach to philosophizing with his analysis of *custom* in the *Enquiries Concerning Human Understanding* (Wiredu 1980c, 169–70).

9. With respect to Aristotle, debate continues over whether his categories were independently conceived or derived from the syntax and semantics of the Greek language.

inaccessible noumenal domain of Kant's transcendental deduction should not be taken too seriously. His point is apparently that via the discipline of biology, the *behavior of a life form to cope and to survive is open to empirical observation.*

At the same time, there is a more generalized form of the genetic approach, summarized by John Dewey: the "genetic method . . . is concerned with the manner or process by which anything comes into experienced existence" (1902, 109). Wiredu puts it this way: "A genetic account of norms [e.g., noncontradiction] is one that seeks to show that they are founded on the empirical constitution and natural antecedents of the human mind. It is, or should be, evident that the basis of all the norms in a given domain cannot itself be a norm but must rather be an existential fact [e.g., survival] of a descriptive nature. Yet, norms will remain norms, whether in logic, epistemology, or ethics" (1996n, 37).

Genetic philosophy is thereby distinguished by the practice that it goes deeper into human being than what is conventional in analytic philosophy. *Language,* for example, can now be treated as part of the (cultural) environment by which one can be conditioned. Once one appreciates this, there are any number of passages in Wiredu's writings where his genetic efforts to identify such *fundamentals of human understanding* are paired with or supplementary to his applications of linguistic analysis.[10] Complicating things is the fact that he does not always explicitly identify argumentation as specifically analytic or genetic in character. Efforts to do so in this text are therefore to be taken with a grain of salt.

Something that should be obvious is that the consequences of a genetic approach will take Wiredu far beyond the confines of the analytic tradition. "But the concepts and structures must be there *before* they can be analysed, and when they are at the *foundations of human thought* philosophy cannot take their existence for granted; it must seek an *explanation of that existence.* That can only be by a *genetic* inquiry. So *philosophy must be both genetic and analytic*" (2002b, 331; my emphasis).

---

10. Wiredu apparently never uses the expression *genetic analysis.*

Two languages Wiredu proposes to compare genetically—focusing on how they are employed to express preferred and supposedly real fundamentals of existence—are English and Twi, a language of the Akan people of Ghana. Let's begin with Wiredu's overview of *natural language* generally and the role he sees himself playing as a philosopher of language:

> There is a further, more pertinent way in which *cultural considerations* may be relevant to—though not determinants of—philosophical theories. I refer to *the effect of language on philosophical thinking*. The nature of a given philosophical position may be influenced by the structure and other characteristics of the language in which it is formulated, and may derive plausibility from the *form* itself of the expression. Here is a good reason for extra vigilance on the part of an African who studies foreign philosophies in foreign languages. *When we learn a new natural language we also, to a certain extent, learn a philosophy.* For the most part *this goes on unconsciously.* But *it is part of the function of philosophers to elicit the general conceptions buried under the forms and turnings of a given language for critical examination.* For this, a certain degree of linguistic detachment is obviously needful though not easily attained. Such detachment may, perhaps, come more easily to foreign speakers of a language [Wiredu presumably has in mind his own relationship with the English language] than the natives so that the African student may be able to avoid the *philosophical pulls of English which native speakers of the language may resist only with difficulty or not at all.*[11] An African student is in quite a strong position in this respect. (1980a, 34; my emphasis)

It is understandable that Western philosophers favor the natural languages of their native cultures for their abstract thinking. By birth a Twi-language speaker, Wiredu is able to approach the syntax and semantics of the English language as an outsider.[12] When paired with

---

11. If readers find it odd that the word "native" is used to reference Westerners, that is further evidence that the population of Africa was described using selective terminology.

12. Syntax refers to the grammar of a language as well as sentence structure and the various parts of speech. Semantics refers to vocabulary.

his special training as a linguistic philosopher, this enables him to identify distinctive characteristics and peculiarities of the English language of which native speakers of that language may not be aware. The foundational character of Wiredu's argumentation here is distinctive and therefore genetic in character. Rather than remain on the level of natural languages and their concepts, as analytic philosophers do, he will attempt to go deeper and demonstrate that, for example, *the syntax of a given language favors certain philosophical prepossessions that can affect abstract thought.*

Wiredu tells us that it is the philosopher's responsibility to study these sorts of things and determine whether and how a person's natural language thereby affects one's philosophical thinking:

> Not having conducted his [Wiredu's] philosophical studies in his own language [at Oxford being trained via the English language], he may the more easily maintain a critical perspective on the philosophical intimations of his own language [in his case Twi]. *He can, moreover, check the philosophical prepossessions of, say, the English language against those of his own.* The balance that is likely to accrue should be an aid to sober reflection.[13] In all this, what is clearly to be emphasized is that, *by taking philosophical cognizance of his own language,* an African philosopher might bring an added dimension to his theoretical considerations. (1980a, 34; my emphasis)

Focusing more narrowly upon the effects of natural languages on philosophical thinking and resuming his critique of Quine, Wiredu will now suggest that Quine himself is a victim of the *"philosophical pulls* of English which native speakers of the language may resist only with difficulty or not at all" (1980a, 34; my emphasis).

Quine did write philosophy primarily in the English language. In which case, how might that language, perhaps even unconsciously, influence philosophers' thinking?

> The English language, for instance, may, by virtue of the special character of its syntax and vocabulary, *create certain initial*

---

13. A similar argument is made for social anthropologists not being natives of the cultures they study.

philosophical prepossessions in the minds of the philosophers
who speak it and think in it. It seems to me, for example, that the
metaphysic of abstract entities (Platonistically construed) or of
substance and attribute or of *mind body dualism* owes any preliminary
plausibility it may appear to have to *contingencies* of this sort.
(Wiredu 1996f, 153; my emphasis)[14]

If Wiredu is challenging the *universality* of these well-known topics
and associated problems of academic philosophy, this is a remarkable
statement. But that is precisely what he is doing. Wiredu will later describe such problems as *tongue-dependent*. By this, he means they arise
from unique features of the grammars and vocabularies of specific
natural languages (e.g., English). They are therefore not universal to
all language cultures.

Wiredu finds the English language distinctive for its use of nouns,
especially *abstract nouns*. A philosopher who is a native speaker of
the language may be inclined to regard the noun form as not just a
normal part of speech but also an appropriate or even natural way of
naming the components of the world, as foundational components of
a philosophical ontology. Wiredu is suggesting that Quine, as a native English-language speaker, is someone who has been *linguistically
conditioned* to favor nouns, particularly abstract nouns and the things
or objects they supposedly name, as ontological building blocks of a
theoretical universe.

The English-language dictionary definition of "noun" is straightforward: "word used as name of person or thing" (*Concise Oxford
English Dictionary* 1964, 824). In that language, nouns are also characterized as substantives, a term that is still used to imply existence.[15]
Persons or things can be *objects*, which the dictionary defines as "thing
placed before eyes or presented to sense, material thing" (*Concise*

---

14. See his discussions of substance-attribute theory and the mind-body
problem later in this chapter. Wiredu 1987a; 1996d, 96–98.

15. Wiredu mentions Aristotle, Descartes, Leibniz, Spinoza, Locke,
Berkeley, and Hume as thinkers who struggled to come to terms with
substance because of the syntax and semantics of the English, French, Greek,
or Latin languages (1996d, 96–98).

Oxford English Dictionary 1964, 830). The combined effects of these meanings, Wiredu suggests, is to incline philosophers like Quine to follow his native language's disposition to describe the world as composed in part of the (physical and abstract) *objects* with which *noun* forms are associated.

Various types of these abstract objects, as is the case with physical objects, thereby take on the status of things that are real with a status, in Wiredu's view, a bit like Plato's forms. "The *unitary abstract noun* is apt to incline some speakers to *objectual* deductions. . . . English has the procedure of forming abstract nouns from 'concrete' ones. Thus, from, for example, 'chair' you get 'chairness'. Adjectives also can yield abstract nouns in a similar manner: 'Red', for example, gives you 'redness'" (1996b, 24). Qualities and attributes become ontological complications because of the propensity to treat them as things (using nouns) that then need their own special space. This is not something Quine had to do. He could have resisted: "There is no lack of English philosophers who are able to resist the ontological suggestiveness of their own vocabulary" (1980a, 35).[16]

There are natural languages other than English that promote alternative approaches to abstractions or universals. This is the transition point at which Wiredu, up to now writing from the vantage point of the English language, begins to focus on the Twi language:

> To make this more concrete, consider the following contrast
> between the English language and Twi, the language of the Akan
> of Ghana. The former has a superabundance of *abstract nouns*, the
> latter dispenses almost completely with that grammatical category,
> expressing abstractions by means of *gerunds* and various *periphrastic*
> expedients.[17] Not surprisingly, one can say such a thing as *universals*
> *are a species of objects* with considerable show of plausibility in

---

16. Appropriately, one of the introductory quotes to Quine's *Word and Object*, attributed to James Grier Miller, is "Ontology recapitulates philology."

17. In the English language, a gerund is formed by adding -*ing* to a verb, as in *reasoning* rather than *to reason*. Periphrasis is a roundabout or indirect way of speaking, or using a phrase to express a meaning rather than a single word, as in "our Father who art in heaven" rather than "God."

English [thinking of Quine]. *Translate it into Twi, and it fails even of a preliminary plausibility.* (1980a, 34; my emphasis)

With respect to so-called parts of speech or the basic syntactical components of the two languages, English favors *nouns*, whereas Twi favors *gerunds*.[18]

> On the other hand, in my own language, the Akan [Twi] language
> spoken in parts of Ghana, the thought transitions represented
> by these English grammatical transformations [creating abstract
> nouns from concrete nouns] are handled quite disanalogically.
> The word for chair is *akongua*, but what corresponds to chairness
> [the abstraction] is not a single word belonging to a separate
> grammatical category, but rather a periphrasis [see fn. 17]. We would
> say something like "the circumstance of something *being* a chair"
> (*se bribi ye akongua*) or if it comes to that, something like "the *being*
> a chair" (*akongua ye*). Here now is the point of this example. In a
> language like Akan, it is obviously going to be very hard for anybody
> to persuade himself, let alone anybody else, of the plausibility of
> saying something like "Chairness is an *abstract object* existing over
> and above particular chairs." (1996b, 24)

Note the inclusion of the gerund *being*, which Wiredu factors into the previous passage.

One consequence for Quine's approach to classes or abstract objects is obvious: they resist translation into the Twi language. In the following passage, English-language nouns are featured as names that can apply to individual physical objects and to abstractions.

> The point is rather that in English and languages like English in
> this respect the fact that, in addition to the periphrastic rendering,
> there is the *unitary abstract noun* is apt to incline some speakers
> to *objectual deductions*, whereas in languages like Akan [Twi]
> there is a distinct disincentive to such *objectivization*—I do not

---

18. If Twi meanings are more accurately conveyed by English-language gerunds, one wonders whether a philosopher writing in Twi would entertain a world of processes. In that case, Twi might be of special interest to process philosophers.

say hypostatization for I do not want to beg the question in favor of the Akan [Twi] language.[19] What I want to do is to emphasize the sharpness of the present contrast between the two languages [presence or absence of abstract nouns]. To this purpose, one might even characterize the contrast by saying that the sentence "Chairness is an abstract *object* existing over and above particular chairs" is *untranslatable* into Akan. (1996b, 24; my emphasis)[20]

The relative absence of abstract nouns does not mean there is a relative absence of *abstract thought* on the part of people who think in the Twi language: "In general, the Akan [Twi] language, as apparently many an African language is very economical in abstract nouns, preferring gerundive and other periphrastic devices.[21] From this it has sometimes been inferred—absurdly—that *Africans tend not to think in abstract terms*. In fact, periphrases can be as abstract as single-word abstract nouns" (1996e, 123). Twi therefore does not have to deal with the problematic or indeterminate ontological status of its abstractions, as is the case with Quine and his English-language ontology of objects:

> [In Twi/Akan,] everything that exists exists in exactly the same sense as everything else. And this sense is *empirical*, broadly speaking. In the Akan [Twi] language to exist is to *wo ho*, which, in literal translation, means "to be at some place". There is no equivalent, in Akan [Twi], of the existential [abstract] "to be" or "is" of English, and there is no way of pretending in that medium to be speaking of the existence of something which is not in space. The *locative* connotation of the Akan [Twi] concept of *existence* is irreducible except metaphorically.[22] Thus you might speak of there existing an explanation for something (*ne nkyerease wo ho*)

---

19. Hypostatization is treating something meant by a word as real without sufficient justification.

20. See also the discussion of untranslatability in chapter 3.

21. One wonders about the evidential basis for this generalization.

22. "Locative" means having a place, a location. "I am aware of the objection that a locative conception of existence will have to be dumb [mute] in respect of the existence of abstract objects like, say numbers. My reply is that abstract objects are objects only in a figurative sense, and figurative locations are not hard to come by" (1996k, 224n14).

without incurring any obligation of spatial specification, because an
explanation is not an *object* in any but a metaphorical sense, and to a
metaphorical object corresponds only a *metaphorical* kind of space.
The same applies to the existence of all so-called *abstract* entities. . . .
it follows that talk of any transcendent being is not just false but
unintelligible, from an Akan [Twi] point of view. (1996c, 49–50; my
emphasis)

In a later publication, Wiredu expands upon this idea of a *common
space* to again challenge the division created by philosophers between
substance and *attribute*, between physical *objects* and the *properties* or
qualities attributed to them. The objects (a chair) are there, situated in
the real world. But their properties or qualities (the chair is red) are
not. They are somehow abstracted from that world and placed in an
entirely different and nonphysical realm of abstractions, universals,
or Quine's classes:

It is not clear why the structure of *thought* and *discourse* has
to be duplicated in the structure of *reality*. Yet *this ontological
interpretation of a semantic distinction* has become widely received
into philosophical and semiphilosophical discourse (in the West).
In English, for example, one speaks of a *thing* and its *properties* or
qualities, and it is frequently taken for granted that a thing belongs
to an ontological order distinct from that of its properties. A thing
is *concrete*, but its properties are *abstract*. . . . The metaphysical
distinction between a thing and its properties *cannot be expressed
in Akan* [Twi] *without unconcealed absurdities.* (1996d, 97–98; my
emphasis)

In later publications, Wiredu will describe this propensity of Akan/
Twi to avoid such ontological complications as *empiricalism* (2011,
31–33).

The *mind-body problem* arises when the thinking or thought that
distinguishes consciousness is defined as essentially and substantially
different from the physical body of which human beings also are composed. If thought is then attributed to an *immaterial mental substance*
(noun) that does not occupy space, as in the case of Descartes, the
ontological complications that follow give rise to the mind-body

problem. For Wiredu, this is another *tongue-dependent* problem that does not deserve to be treated as common or universal to all language cultures. Given Western languages' dependence on *nouns as foundational to understanding* and their associations with substances or objects, Western philosophers were predisposed to regard *mind* as some sort of substance or object that, paradoxically, did not occupy space. "In the Akan [Twi] language the word for 'thought' is the same as the word for 'mind'; it is *adwene* in both cases. My own interpretation of this, and also of Akan usage generally, is that the conception of 'mind' implicit here is of mind as a *function* rather than an *entity*. Mind, in this conception, is the function of thought" (1996a, 16; my emphasis).

In his view, which is inspired by the Twi language, *mind* as *thought* and *thinking* is a kind of *activity* that is better regarded as a purely *conceptual* enterprise. Treating it as a substance, entity, or object makes it nonconceptual. Joining the conceptual to the nonconceptual becomes what philosophers describe as a category mistake—combining two different kinds of things that should not be combined because they are by definition essentially different from one another (Wiredu 1987a, 164). It would also seem his *empiricalism*, which censures the creation of abstractions (mind) that then exist in a nonphysical manner that is difficult to define, would reject treating mind as some sort of special substance.

In these comparative analyses, Twi is not being treated as a language indicative of underdeveloped intellects or of a tribal or traditional people—all words with pejorative implications. It is treated, simply, as a *different* language. Why is it that the English language must continue to exercise so dominant a role in academic philosophy? Its grammar and vocabulary, whether on ordinary or second-order levels, have become implied paradigms that other language cultures should emulate if they are to secure philosophical merit. This was one solid reason for Wiredu putting elements of this argument into an essay entitled "On an African Orientation in Philosophy." Even today in academic philosophy, indigenous African languages are often ignored, perhaps because they are still assumed to be less sophisticated and therefore of less philosophical prepossession than their Western counterparts.

Wiredu's original analyses are meant to prove that understanding should be achieved on the basis of concrete comparisons rather than presuppositions or insinuations about people's intellectual proficiency. "It would, of course, be a kind of genetic fallacy to suppose simply because a given doctrine is encouraged by the characteristics of a foreign language it is false.[23] And an African would be guilty of a fallacy hardly less egregious if she were to think that the philosophical preconceptions inspired by her own vernacular are sound simply on account of that provenance" (1996f, 226n15).

A proper relationship between philosophy and natural languages occurs when "a philosophical suggestion emanating from considerations relating to a natural language . . . [is] demonstrable or supportable with *arguments not depending on peculiarities of the original language*" (1996h, 207; my emphasis). Languages can be mined for original and potentially valuable philosophical *prepossessions* or *intimations*. But elaboration, evaluation, and justification must then be provided by *independent argumentation*. This is what Wiredu would insist he has been doing via his analytic and genetic concerns with the English and Twi languages in this chapter and elsewhere.

---

23. "Genetic" here refers to a specific type of informal logical fallacy, not to be confused with Wiredu's use of the term.

THREE

~~~

On Translation

THE *PROBLEM OF UNIVERSALS THAT* was discussed in chapter 1 concerned the part they should play in *ontology*—whether they are things that somehow exist in the real world. In this chapter, the question is whether they play a part in *language.* Are there a significant number of *concepts* that natural languages share in common?[1] If there are such *meanings* that cross cultures, this would obviously have positive consequences for translations between natural languages. In the "Logic and Ontology" articles, Wiredu does not directly address the issue of these kinds of universals. The viability of *intercultural translation* becomes another activity that qualifies for a genetic approach in his later publications. Wiredu has a good deal to say about this in an essay entitled "Are There Cultural Universals?" (1996b).[2] He argues

---

1. In academic philosophy, the term *proposition* is used to describe the meanings that are shared in common by statements that basically say the same thing in different natural languages; for example, "I am hungry" in English, "j'ai faim" in French, or "ebí ńpa mi" in Yorùbá.

2. One might expect him to use the word *cognitive* rather than the word *cultural.* This perhaps indicates that Wiredu recognizes that linguistic fluency alone is not enough to ensure insightful understanding of another culture. Cultural fluency is required for communication that results in real understanding.

33

that the *evidence* clearly indicates universals do play an important role in language learning and intercultural communication. These are the experiences in which we encounter them and come to realize they do underlie human languages generally:

> No human language is known which non-native speakers cannot, in principle, learn as a second language. The reason underlying this fact is that *language is a system of skills fundamental to being human*. These are the skills of *reflective perception, abstraction*, and *inference*. By means of the first skill one can, in principle, re-identify any symbol and its possible referent; by means of the second, one can, in principle, understand any semantic structures and classifications, analyzing composites and synthesizing units as the case may require, and by means of the third, one can, in principle, map out the bearing of any given proposition on (at least some) close or remote consequences. In sum, a human being is a *rule-following animal*, and *language is nothing but an arrangement of rules*. Therefore, barring the impairment of faculties, any human being will necessarily have the capacity to understand and use a language, and *if one can understand any one language, one can understand any language*. (1996b, 25; my emphasis)

Somewhat ironically, the example of a universal concept that Wiredu first chooses to discuss is that of the "object."

> The concept of object in general is a common possession of all humans. Operating with this concept is an essential aspect of the human way of interacting with the environment. It is what gives it a cognitive dimension. And because a basic imperative of this cognitive interaction is *the drive for self-preservation and equilibrium, the essential discrimination of items of the environment*, which the possession of the concept of object in general makes possible, *will be of the same basic kind in actuality, if not necessity in articulation, among all humankind. These essential discriminations will obviously be of the objects of direct perception.* The word "direct" here does not imply the absence of conceptualization. But *at this level* there is a basic similarity among humans by dint of semi-instinctual constraints. For this reason, the nearer a set of items of discrimination is to *direct perception* the easier it will be to correlate its elements with

the different systems of symbolization obtaining among different peoples. This is what ensures that all human languages are, at bottom, inter-learnable and inter-translatable. (1996b, 25–26; my emphasis)

This is not the same English-language meaning of "object" he criticizes Quine for prioritizing in chapter 1. This is the genetically minded Wiredu who has in mind the *foundational* experience of individuation, discrimination, or singling out that enables us to differentiate and then speak of individual things or objects as parts of our experience. Whether we then go on to describe and explain them using nouns or gerunds is a different issue. Quine also discusses this foundational level to experience at length in *Word and Object* (1960) and *Theories and Things* (1981).

More important to the genetic Wiredu than universal concepts or, for that matter, languages are the underlying *faculties* of human beings that make them possible and give rise to languages. He refers to the italicized abilities in the above passage—reflective perception, abstraction, and inference—as "epistemic universals" and says they are definitive of the common humanity that makes possible all of the languages and concepts we use to communicate with one another. Use of a genetic approach here enables him to go beyond the diversity of languages and identify the fundamental human faculties that give rise to them. This can also be seen as a step in his campaign to endorse a *common humanity* by focusing on the essentials that we share. "Whether the difficulty in communication occurs within one culture or between different cultures, because human beings are rule-following animals and because we all, by and large, stand on the same cognitive pedestal of sensible perception, such difficulties can sometimes be overcome, or if not overcome, at least, reduced to something less than impenetrability" (Wiredu 1996b, 26).

There must be a place for *abstract concepts* that are culturally particular, that are *unique* to a particular natural language. They are not likely to be so prevalent as to prohibit communication, but a particularly obscure concept might require an explanatory monograph or even entire book in order to be adequately translated into and explained in a foreign language.[3] There may be *logical differences*, but they too can be accommodated: "Even if certain cognitive rules used in one culture are not used in another, there is no reason to discount the possibility of there being fundamental rules common to both (and, possibly, all) cultures in terms of which the rules in question might be evaluated cross-culturally" (Wiredu 1995, 135–36; see also Wiredu 1996d, 84–85, 214n6). Such texts can be produced by bilingual philosophers, anthropologists, linguists, and others. But it is those *deeper faculties that a genetic account highlights* that make this possible. This is the more important point: "What is it that unifies us? . . . It is our biological cultural identity as *homines sapientes*. . . . we are organisms that go beyond instinct in the drive for equilibrium and self-preservation in specific ways, namely, by means of reflective perception, abstraction, deduction and induction" (1996b, 22; my emphasis in part).

W. V. O. Quine deserves some consideration for his views regarding *universals* and the consequences for *translating* between languages. At this point, relatively trouble-free translation seems to be something Wiredu is taking for granted. Quine saw translation between natural languages generally as a difficult and arbitrary process by which cultures could be victimized. This is one point of his *indeterminacy thesis of radical translation*. It is not to be confused with the other thesis concerning existence that was discussed in chapter 1. The indeterminacy thesis (IT) is something else, and it remains one of the more fiercely debated major-minor issues of academic philosophy.[4] Its critics are numerous, and the critical interpretations and attempted refutations it has engendered comprise a substantial body of literature.[5] Today,

---

3. For an example involving an African language, see the elucidations of the Luo concept of "juok" or "jok" in Masolo (2010). For a comparable English language analysis of "belief" as an odd-job word, see Needham (1972).

4. The philosopher Hilary Putnam has remarked, "Chapter 2 of Quine's *Word and Object* [where Quine introduces the indeterminacy thesis] contains what may well be the most fascinating and the most discussed philosophical argument since Kant's Transcendental Deduction of the Categories" (Putnam 1975, 159).

5. A comprehensive bibliography of major interpretations, criticisms, elaborations, and defenses of the IT is to be found in Kirk (1986, 259–65),

its controversial status endures, in no small part because of Quine's sustained efforts over the years to elaborate the thesis in a continuing dialogue with his critics. Recasting the technical philosophical arguments of the IT into severely shortened, summary form can be dangerous. The issues involved can become more simplistic than is the case, and this tends to disproportionately dramatize some of the paradoxical, counterintuitive consequences of the thesis.[6] Perhaps the best way to proceed would be to ask readers to view the IT as providing *alternative views of language* that will enable them to experiment with and thereby consider some of the interesting consequences that follow for the *translation* of alien beliefs and abstract ideas.

The aim of the following summary is to highlight some of Quine's insights about the nature of language and the relationships between languages that arise from the IT.[7]

1. Let's begin by regarding each natural language (English, Chinese, Twi, Swahili, etc.) as a unique human creation that has its own intricate

---

updated in Kirk (2004). A much-quoted informal discussion of the IT by many of the principals involved (including Quine), remarkable for its plain talk about complex philosophical issues, is to be found in Davidson and Hintikka (2012).

6. Those who are interested in a more detailed examination of the IT, with specific reference to possible consequences for African philosophy, are referred to Hallen and Sodipo (1997), chapter 1: "Indeterminacy and the Translation of Alien Behaviour."

7. In the literature of African philosophy, an early reference to the IT occurs in a footnote to Maurier (1984). Interestingly, the footnote is editorial, added to Maurier's text by Richard Wright. It contains an explicit recommendation that the issues raised by the IT should warrant the special interest of African philosophers. I am indebted to Robin Horton for first drawing my attention to Quine's IT, and for many invaluable conversations about translation. Horton's collected thoughts on the subject are available in Horton (1993).

There was substantial discussion of the IT in the philosophy of the social sciences and in anthropology before it became an issue for African philosophy. A particularly informative interdisciplinary collection is to be found in Hollis and Lukes (1982).

conceptual network(s)—ontological, epistemological, aesthetic, and so forth—with distinctive forms of expression. Our immediate experience of the world is not self-explanatory or neatly categorized. It is humankind, by means of its creative genius, that invents languages and imposes empirical and theoretical order on that experience. As Quine describes language at one point: "In an obvious way this structure of interconnected sentences is a single connected fabric including all sciences, and indeed everything we ever say about the world; for the logical truths at least, and no doubt many more commonplace sentences too, are germane to all topics and thus provide connections" (Quine 1960, 12–13).

2. Let's also suspend our tendency to assume that in their heart of hearts, all of our languages share in common a group of *universal meanings* or propositions. By universal propositions, Quine refers to the belief that although the word for "destiny" may be different in Twi from what it is in English, the underlying meaning is the same. Quine's view is not specifically a defense of relativism. It is a critique of the idea that we have any direct 'experience' of universal meanings.[8]

This is the Quine who will dismiss the whole idea of *meanings* as entirely "ill-suited for use as an instrument of philosophical clarification and analysis" (1981, 185) in chapter 4. Why, then, does he write of meanings here as if important components of our understanding? He does so because people who deal with languages and translation talk about meanings all the time, talk about them as if they are real. Quine wants to communicate with those people and therefore temporarily adopts their vernacular.

3. A belief in the universality of meanings may be of empathic value to someone who is a stranger to another language-culture, or of heuristic value to the lexicographer devising a bilingual dictionary, but it tends to negate the possibility of creative uniqueness with which we began. It can also be said to promote a form of ethnocentrism, in that a translator who believes in universal propositions or does translation

---

8. J. J. Katz (1988) compares the severity of the effects of Quine's critique of meaning to those of Hume's skeptical critique of causality.

between two languages as if there are universal propositions will likely favor the meanings of his or her own natural language—English, for example—effectively universalizing them into propositions, and then proceed to *impose* English meanings upon other languages via the process of translation.

4. Let's therefore suspend our conventional notion of *meaning*. When an English-language translator sets out to communicate with an alien, the psychological predispositions of her own language may subliminally persuade her to conceive of the inner alien person as a *mind*, as a consciousness inhabiting a body. They may also persuade the translator to presume that consciousness contains the meanings that she needs to reach and to study in order to formulate accurate translations of the alien language. Worse still, the translator may be deceived into thinking that the translations of alien meanings that she eventually does propose derive their accuracy from the fact that they really do correspond to meanings in the alien mind.

In fact, we never have direct access to another consciousness. What we do have direct access to are alien words coming out of alien mouths. Strictly from a methodological point of view, therefore, it is deceptive for the translator to operate in anything other than a *behavioristic* universe. For those who are not familiar with behaviorism, it contends that in order to be empirically or scientifically minded, we should avoid theories based upon experience that is *subjective*. Comparatively internal or personal experiences involving things like the mind, ideas, thoughts, feelings, and so forth are therefore ruled out for theoretical purposes. Rather than the subjective experience of hope, for example, behaviorism asks us to focus on the relevant behavior—verbal utterances and physical demeanor of someone who is hoping—that can be empirically observed. It is important to say that the form of behaviorism being introduced here is methodological rather than the reductive psychological species enunciated by B. F. Skinner (1992). Quine is not denying the existence of the conscious mental self, of personal feelings, or of introspection. But these experiences are private to each individual rather than public, and therefore they are of limited value for philosophizing that prioritizes empirical evidence.

5. Familiarity with an alien language on the relatively *empirical* level is not sufficient to enable us to *predict* the nature of alien theoretical or *abstract* beliefs. The gap between the accidental spilling of salt and the beliefs that interpret it as bad luck is vast. The gap between being involved in an accident and the beliefs that interpret it as part of one's destiny also is vast.

6. The hopes for objectivity, for proof of accuracy in translation, differ substantially between the relatively empirical ("It is raining") and the abstract ("Truth is beauty"). Translations of empirical statements are susceptible to a degree of public, verifiable testing of meaning. Theoretical abstractions are relatively immaterial in character. Translation on the abstract level is accordingly much more difficult to control or to verify.

7. Translators who are *bilingual* do not avoid these problems. They may be perfectly fluent in each of the languages that are targeted by a particular bilingual translation. But when they claim that a certain term extracted from one of the languages means precisely the same as a certain term in the other language, they are still imposing the meanings of the one language's conceptual network upon the other in hypothetical fashion.

8. Any extensive English-language translation process as found, for example, in a work of cultural anthropology, cross-cultural philosophy, or a bilingual dictionary is an elaborate, interrelated network constructed of innumerable hypotheses that stipulate the meanings of English-language words as equivalent to alien-language words. Each definition of an alien word becomes, in effect, an *interpretation* rather than a translation, a working hypothesis, a rendering based upon a network of other translated renderings.[9]

Looking at things from the perspective of the IT, the approximate nature of the entire translation process is made manifest. There is also the possibility that another translator could come along who would disagree with the schema worked out by a predecessor and introduce an alternative schema, an alternative interpretation, that differed in

---

9. The contending translations of the Christian Bible provide noteworthy examples.

important respects and therefore would produce a different version of the alien beliefs in translation.

9. What objective criteria can one appeal to in order to determine which alternative translation is determinate—that is, is closest to the true (alien) meanings? *There are none* that would be sufficient. This, admittedly in summary form, is the point of Quine's IT.

In the absence of secure objective criteria for determining which translation schema is more accurate, Quine proposes several *guidelines* that he thinks may at least reduce the risks of producing translations of alien meanings that are offensive as well as indeterminate.[10] Some consequences of these alternative criteria are as follows. One would become suspicious of translations of alien meanings that propose to assign a *plurality* of meanings to the same term in an alien conceptual system. A translator might try to justify this by saying that the meaning involved is dependent upon the circumstances or the contexts in which the term is used. Given indeterminacy, an alternative reason could be that translators have tactical recourse to *context-dependent meanings* because they—perhaps unwittingly or unknowingly—have been unsuccessful in coming up with a determinate meaning. In effect, then, the translators attribute their own confusion to the alien conceptual system. This can make the aliens appear somehow exotic or bizarre when in fact the real culprit is the translation.

Suspicion should also be focused upon cases in which the alien is made to mean something empirically *bizarre and inappropriate* to a situation's common-sense circumstances. This may indicate a situation in which inadequate translation results in aliens apparently affirming transparently false statements and therefore becoming less than rational. Given indeterminacy, an alternative explanation could be that there are problems in the conceptual translation network that cause alien meanings to take on apparent absurdity in the language of translation.

Quine is not advocating a ban on translation or communication across cultures and languages. He very much appreciates this is taking

---

10. Quine 1960, 73–79; Hallen and Sodipo 1997, 30–34.

place all the time. Neither is he implying that published studies of alien abstract beliefs that are based upon translations of alien languages are necessarily false. Quine is advocating a degree of *skepticism* about purportedly rigorous, objective, detailed analyses of alien abstract ideas in translation. Once one recognizes the weakness of the empirical constraints placed upon communications between two languages that may historically have no cause to share a single cognate in common, what exactly is the objective basis upon which we assign virtually literal accuracy to theoretical translations?[11]

From the standpoint of indeterminacy, studies of alien abstract meanings in translation are built upon a more fragile basis of interpretation than their rhetoric implies. This needs to be recognized more widely than it is, especially when such studies serve as an empirical basis for attributing oddities in reasoning and/or theoretical understanding to an alien conceptual system. A prelogical mentality could be the creation of a prelogical translation. One who is persuaded by the possibility of indeterminacy would prefer that we be more flexible, *more open to the possibilities of misrepresentation* and approximation by translation, especially on the level of abstract thought. On this level, there may be no such thing as literal translation. Everything becomes relatively free translation, interpretation.

To conclude these remarks on the IT, Quine is not saying that people must always be portrayed as rational. His skepticism about the entire process of translating the meanings from one language into another moves him to caution us that we have as good reason to suspect our systems of translation as we do to suspect the alien of being responsible for apparently exotic, bizarre, or irrational statements in any given context.

Wiredu is not a behaviorist and will not endorse Quine's rejection of meanings as impossibly subjective. In fact, in chapter 4 he will insist upon *meanings* as components of his own epistemology. Wiredu makes reference to Quine's IT in an essay entitled "On Defining

---

11. Cognates are words in different languages that share the same root of origin—e.g., "family" (English) and "familia" (Spanish), which derive from the earlier Latin "famiglia."

African Philosophy" (1991). In this essay, in the course of a discussion about possible differences between African and Western conceptual systems, Wiredu remarks, "The thesis of the indeterminacy of radical translation advanced by the logician and philosopher W. V. Quine in his *Word and Object* is of the greatest interest in this context" (1991, 101).[12] In an accompanying footnote (109n42), he asks, without answering, whether the thesis effectively undermines all translation between natural languages, by which he apparently means on both the empirical and abstract levels.

There is an additional remark in footnote 42 that plays upon the word "radical" but is meant to be taken seriously: *"As for 'radical' translation, God knows that African thought has suffered enough from it."* By reading between the quotation marks, it is possible to understand something of what he means. Bear in mind his efforts to defend the African intellectual heritage from scholars who have portrayed Africa's cultures as intellectually inferior. Their writings can be construed as radical in that they incorporate serious misunderstandings. Such misunderstandings could certainly involve mistranslations. Would Wiredu then agree that some of these mistranslations could be linked to indeterminacy as well as misunderstandings and prejudice?

Wiredu can agree with Quine that the more abstract concepts are, the harder they can become to understand, much less translate.

> The *difficulties of intelligibility and translation* among humans are due principally to the changes and chances to which the twin procedures of *abstraction* and *inference* are subjects in this world. It is through these processes that human beings make their semantic ascents from the pedestal of direct sensible perception to the heights of sophisticated theoretical conceptions or into the clouds of conceptual obscurity and confusion. . . . In fact, when the concepts

---

12. The context he has in mind is relativism—whether the meanings of fundamental concepts like *truth* can be relative to different natural languages. Wiredu refers directly to the philosophical analyses of the Yoruba language by Hallen and Sodipo (1997). They found that the perfectly reasonable criteria governing use of the term òótọ́ make its meaning fundamentally different from the English-language *true* and therefore relative to that language culture.

in question are highly abstract and basic to a world view, this lack of equation [clear meaning equivalents between different languages] reveals the root of all philosophy or, at any rate, much of it. (Wiredu 1996b, 26–27; my emphasis)

If the meanings of abstract terms are in need of clarification and justification, they may qualify as additional candidates for the discipline of philosophy.

Despite indeterminacy, Quine does allow for the possibility that an alien can achieve the same level of fluency in a foreign language as natives of that language culture.[13]

The linguist who is serious ... will steep himself in the language, disdainful of English parallels, to the point of speaking it like a native. His learning of it even from the beginning can have been as free of all thought of other languages as you please; it can have been virtually an accelerated counterpart of infantile learning. When at length he does turn his hand to translation ... he can do so as a bilingual. (Quine 1959, 474–75).[14]

According to Quine, where such a *bilingual* person will encounter indeterminacy is when they propose to translate between two languages in which they enjoy fluency. Achieving fluency in the languages is one thing, but translating between them is another. Quine argues that bilinguals err if they translate with the presumption that meaning synonymy is true. In effect, they are stipulating or imposing the meanings of one language for or upon the other.

A question worth asking is whether this would apply to Wiredu's translations of Twi meanings in his English-language texts. He does acknowledge there can be a degree of what he terms "untranslatability" when working between languages: "the ability to perceive the

---

13. There's an amusing scene in Lawrence Durrell's *Alexandria Quartet* (1991) when a French diplomat looks at his watch during a dinner party and realizes he is late for another appointment. He rushes from the scene while exclaiming, in his elementary English, "I am retarded, I am retarded!" "Retardé" happens to be French for the English-language "late."

14. Wiredu comments approvingly on this point by Quine (Wiredu 1996b, 25).

untranslatability of an expression from one language into another is a mark of [superior] linguistic understanding" (1996b, 25; my emphasis). But he sees it in a positive light, in that it requires a degree of linguistic sophistication and sensitivity that is not consistent with the IT.[15] He then goes on to say that "untranslatability, then, can be a problem but it does not necessarily argue unintelligibility (1996b, 25)" or indeterminacy.[16] This kind of understanding apparently means that translators can recognize that a concept in a language they speak fluently would be very difficult to translate into another language in which they also are fluent.

Wiredu's description of bilingualism, with a critical philosophical potential, underscores his differences with Quine:

> Because of the self-reflexivity of *philosophical thinking*, we can "step outside" our own conceptual frameworks [languages] and examine them critically . . . we can use the English language to "step outside" the very same language and study its syntax and semantics.
>
> Be that as it may, it should be noted that in order to [learn another language] . . . we do not need to step outside our framework; what we do is to step inside the [new] framework in question. To learn the language . . . is to enter the framework. The thing about this journey is that we can carry our own conceptual framework [for Wiredu, Twi] along with us.
>
> It is sometimes supposed . . . that to [learn another language] is to try arbitrarily to *impose* one's ideas and criteria upon [it]. *This is an ill-considered suggestion.* (Wiredu 1995b, 131–32; my emphasis)

What will promote the accuracy of translations between different natural languages—in fact "de-radicalize" it, Wiredu says—is "sustained cultural intercourse." The more two cultures interact, the more the quality of translations between their respective languages will improve (Wiredu 1996d, 216–17n37).

The linguist Benjamin Lee Whorf (2011), and what has come to be known as the Sapir-Whorf hypothesis, were current during the time Wiredu was at Oxford. The hypothesis makes a strong case for

---

15. Must Quine have had it in order to hypothesize indeterminacy?
16. See his initial references to untranslatability in chapter 2.

linguistic relativism. Whorf argues, mainly on the basis of problematic examples of translation, that the concepts of natural languages can differ so fundamentally that people trying to use them would be unable to communicate. An innovation arising from the Sapir-Whorf hypothesis is that it challenges the epistemological presumption that regardless of our eventual differences, we all begin from observing the same natural world as a given. The hypothesis argues the influence of natural languages upon our understanding is so profound and fundamental that there is no longer a shared natural world. Languages even condition us to view their own versions of the natural world.

When Wiredu compares the English language's use of nouns with the Twi language's use of gerunds and then relates this to their differing views of *space*, this would seem to confirm the Sapir-Whorf hypothesis to some degree. But Wiredu would say that the same person is able to transcend, understand, and thereby consciously compare the incompatible views endorsed by the two languages, which would constrain the effects of the absolute relativism associated with the hypothesis. Alternatively, the indeterminacy thesis would challenge and question the presumed determinate understanding of the meanings of the terms involved in such comparisons.

In "Are There Cultural Universals?" Wiredu explicitly disagrees with Whorf about how serious a challenge conceptual differences can pose for understanding between diverse language cultures (1996b, 24–5). He has agreed that there can be concepts that are unique to a language and therefore more difficult to translate, but more important, there are the *conceptual universals that cross cultures and provide a secure basis for translation.* Wiredu's genetic concerns play a role in all of this. It is the sameness that human beings share with respect to their faculties of reflective perception, abstraction, and inference that ultimately ensures their languages also share enough meanings and understanding in common so that intercultural translation can take place.

With respect to the discipline of *epistemology* or theory of knowledge, Quine and Wiredu both endorse *naturalism*, which involves increased reliance upon *science* as a source of information relevant to epistemic issues. Quine is famous for his 1969 publication "Epistemology Naturalized," in which he says the following:

> Epistemology still goes on, though in a new setting and a clarified status. *Epistemology*, or something like it, simply falls into place as a chapter of *psychology* and hence of *natural science*. It studies a natural phenomenon, viz., a physical human subject. This human subject is accorded a certain experimentally controlled input . . . and in the fullness of time the subject delivers as output a description of the three-dimensional external world and its history. The relation between the meager input [via sensation] and the torrential output [highly abstract scientific theories] is a relation that we are prompted to study for somewhat the same reasons that always prompted epistemology; namely, in order to see what evidence relates to *theory*, and in what ways one's theory of nature *transcends* any available *evidence*. (1969a, 82–83; my emphasis)[17]

Wiredu endorses something similar with his repeated references to biology as the discipline that grounds his genetic method: "The mention of the term '*naturalistic*' brings us to an important type of philosophical outlook which may be regarded as the genus of which the *genetic* approach is a species. '*Naturalism*' in philosophy is a broad rubric covering every manner of philosophizing in which explanations and elucidations are developed exclusively in terms of *factors relating to man and external nature*. Thus, obviously, *genetic epistemology is naturalistic*" (1980c, 171; my emphasis).

The most contentious remaining issue between Quine and Wiredu is how Quine would respond to the genetic dissection of his ontology. Is Wiredu treating Quine as a creature with an intellect who had been conditioned by his (linguistic) environment? Quine has suggested that psychology can help to understand how human beings progress from the level of sensation to that of abstraction. A better understanding of how language comes about would be a part of that exercise.

---

17. In *From Stimulus to Science* (1995), Quine is intrigued by a humanity that starts out limited to the five basic senses and a brain yet ends up producing incredibly sophisticated and technical scientific theories about, for example, a universe that is infinite.

A question that Wiredu himself does not discuss is how or why the English language came to favor nouns and the Twi language gerunds. Can a genetic approach help to answer that question, and if so, why doesn't Wiredu address it?

Judging the truth of the conceptual systems of the world's various natural languages in terms of an absolute criterion (which itself would have to be expressed in language) might seem a preposterous enterprise. But if reduced to more manageable proportions—such as, for example, the relative merits and demerits of different systems of epistemological concepts and criteria, when judged as instrumental tools—it does not seem so impossible. Wiredu's genetic epistemology, for example, would seem to be a step in that direction (1980c, 171).

Quine's IT, on the other hand, could sensitize those committed to dealing with the understanding, translation, and assessment of abstract ideas on the basis of cross-cultural comparisons to the limitations of conceptual networks generally for the representation and analysis of alien meanings. And this caution should extend as much to non-Western interpretations of Western meanings, as to Western interpretations of non-Western meanings. But as Wiredu argues against Quine, successful language learning on the part of hundreds of millions of people, translations that can be confirmed by multiple experts, and the discovery rather than the imposition of universal meanings combine to provide seriously empirical evidence of the viability of intercultural and interlinguistic translations.

So far, abstract objects or *universals* have provided a degree of continuity to this text. Whether expressed as nouns (English) or gerunds (Twi) and viewed as objects (Quine) or meanings (Wiredu), the debates involved are relevant to philosophers everywhere. With the contributions from a genetic approach, Wiredu means to introduce an original way of doing philosophy. His references to a "genetic epistemology" represent an effort to involve that philosophical subdiscipline more directly with science, in his case biology. Genetic involves heredity, and Wiredu's aim is to arrive at a better understanding of the origins of our understanding.

Quine's indeterminacy thesis introduces a paradoxical argument that creates problems especially for the representation of theoretical abstractions.[18] Quine might say that Wiredu highlights indeterminacy when he presents examples of the ways in which substantives and abstractions are expressed in Twi and English that are so different as to be untranslatable. Both philosophers operate on a meta level, but one that has empirical foundations and consequences.[19] As for Wiredu, he sets out to demonstrate that African languages can make edifying contributions to the problems of academic philosophy. In doing so, he advances the rather unusual argument that the syntax and semantics of the English language are important determinants of Quine's ontology, which thereby becomes culturally relative and a candidate for his own indeterminacy thesis.[20]

That the problems of philosophy may be traced to genetic considerations is a thesis Wiredu will continue to explore in the chapters that follow. In chapter 4, he will introduce a theory of *truth* that draws upon genetic, academic, philosophical, and African sources.

---

18. "Perhaps the doctrine of indeterminacy of translation will have little air of paradox for readers familiar with Wittgenstein's latter-day remarks on meaning" (Quine 1960, 77n2).

19. Language used to discuss language. This kind of analysis "involves stepping above both [languages], onto a meta-platform so to speak" (Wiredu 1996b, 25).

20. Which leads one to wonder what effect Wiredu's argument would have if applied to scientific knowledge when expressed in and by natural languages. It also reminds one of Quine's concern in chapter 1 to free science from ordinary language by turning to formal logic.

FOUR

~~~

On Truth

OVER THE COURSE OF A person's lifetime, an enormous amount of information will be directed at them by their family, friends and associates, teachers, and the media. How are they to go about determining what portion of that information is more reliable, perhaps even true, and what is less reliable, perhaps even false? Wiredu's interests in these questions will lead him to explore the nature of *truth* as a practical and philosophical concern.

To do this, he will formulate an original *epistemology* or theory of knowledge. But first he must continue and conclude his critique of American philosopher W. V. O. Quine. Quine has advised philosophers to beware of involving philosophy with terminology derived from ordinary language. In everyday life, people are often not concerned to stipulate precise meanings for their words when communicating with one another.[1] An example of such a term that Quine wants to exclude from theoretical philosophy is the word "meaning": "Meaning . . . is a worthy *object* of philosophical and scientific clarification and analysis, [but] . . . it is *ill-suited* for use as an *instrument* of *philosophical* and scientific clarification and *analysis*" (Quine 1981, 185; my emphasis).

---

1. See the Pegasus examples in chapter 1.

Quine's point is that once philosophers are aware of the positives and negatives that follow from allowing this term to play a part in, for example, epistemology, they will appreciate that it is best to avoid use of it altogether. His argument proceeds as follows: Some philosophers are attracted to meanings because they think they can help us understand what is involved when we use words to talk about things. They argue that we choose the words we do because of their meanings. Therefore, meanings deserve to play an important part in the philosophy of language.

Quine wants to ask, If meanings as distinct entities exist and are real, where are they located? Are they inside people—in a place that behaviorism tells us is empirically inaccessible? Behaviorism's rejection of meanings was discussed in chapter 3. Are they outside of people—floating around in the universe somehow, somewhere?[2] If we can't determine a specific location, perhaps it is counterproductive to continue to talk about them as if they have one. Quine thinks the entire process of communicating with words can be clarified and simplified if we talk only about *words* and the *things* they refer to, without adding on meanings as additional things that are real objects in their own right. If we want to know what a word is talking about, we don't need meanings. All we have to do is look at the kind of objects (particular or abstract) that it names. It's therefore best to avoid use of the term altogether.

Wiredu finds this unacceptable and argues that *words without meanings are not words*. They are simply noises that come out of someone's mouth or random marks on a page (1974, 35–38). Words have to have meanings to give them significance. Meanings therefore need to be a part of epistemology, because one grounded exclusively on words without explicit meanings would fail to communicate anything to anyone. This means that the concept "meaning" can be rescued from

---

2. Following upon his genetic study of nouns in the English language, Wiredu can also claim that their influence inclines Quine to approach meanings as objects that by definition would have to be ontologically real. See chapter 2. There is noteworthy similarity between Quine's argument here and that of Wiredu with regard to properties and attributes in chapter 2.

the obscurities of ordinary language and provide philosophy with a valuable and sensible theoretical component.

The model Wiredu arrives at for how we can *talk about* or refer to things in the world has three components: *concepts,* the *meanings* that give them significance, and the *things* in the world they are used to talk about. He does agree that meanings have to have more specific identities and *have to be somewhere.* He has a response to each of these concerns. Words and their meanings are best treated as *concepts,* which are sometimes characterized as objects of thought. And because the concepts of our languages are the creations of human beings, we can say that they exist, most importantly, in the *minds* of human beings.[3] "It is valid . . . to maintain that *concepts exist* nowhere but in the *mind*" (Wiredu 1996a, 16; my emphasis). "It is usual to say that the meaning or significance of an expression [word, etc.] is a *concept,* an *idea,* a *notion,* or more rarely, a *thought* [all associated with minds]" (Wiredu 1975, 30; my emphasis). All of this is unacceptable to Quine because of his behaviorism. Mental experience—consciousness—is private and personal and therefore cannot be shared directly with others. Mind is *subjective,* which means (!) it can provide no basis for the observable, *empirical* verification of claims about it.

There are any number of philosophers who have reservations about linking concepts exclusively to human minds because this makes them and their meanings potentially problematically subjective—at worst, many private minds with potentially many *private meanings.*[4] Wiredu therefore thinks it important to clarify his use of the word "concept." He recognizes the need to mitigate the subjectivity people like Quine use to trash *mind* as a foundational component of epistemology. To begin with, the relationship between a concept and its meaning should not be hard to understand. The word "dog" qualifies as a concept whose meaning is clear. It applies to innumerable animals that constitute a certain class of "quadrupeds of many breeds wild & domesticated" (*Concise Oxford English Dictionary* 1964, 361).

---

3. Ontologically this would apparently mean (!) that if human beings were to disappear from the world, concepts (including universals) would as well.

4. See Wittgenstein (1958) for his discussions of private language.

The subjectivity affecting concepts and their meanings when based in the human mind is more problematic. Wiredu's strategy is to undertake critical revaluations of attributes that he believes have been unfairly exaggerated by philosophers about the differences between the *subjective* and the *objective* (1975, 30–40).

Here are several of the more important points Wiredu makes on the basis of those analyses: In analytic philosophy generally, empirical evidence is favored when it comes to proving something true or false. Being empirical means that evidence can be made available, in principle, to other observers. Because of this, being *empirical* is most often associated with being *objective*: "It seems to be assumed that to be *objective* is to be independent of individual minds, and obversely, that to be dependent on individual minds is to be *subjective*" (1975, 31; my emphasis).

Experience itself proves this distinction to be exaggerated. *Experience is not subjective* if that means that only the individual concerned has access to it: "If to depend on a human *mind* in any way at all is to be *subjective*, then we would have, absurdly, to say that everything we can know is subjective, for our knowledge of things depends partly on the things themselves and partly on *our faculties of knowing* [presumably located in minds]. . . . Yet, we do not say that [everything is subjective]" (1975, 31; my emphasis). Philosophers who prioritize being objective have exaggerated the perils that may follow from placing concepts in the minds of those who are using them to communicate with one another. A person may be an individual, but that does not make them subjective in the sense that statements arising from their experiences are by definition unreliable: "To be dependent on individual minds . . . does not automatically imply being subjective. . . . Even when a statement relates to sensations, it may still be objective" (Wiredu 1975, 30, 32; my emphasis).

Wiredu wants to say that because communication between individual minds must involve concepts and their meanings, certain *standards* have to be observed by the minds involved: "Language is a *system* . . . and its results are interpersonally intelligible because of the *rule-governed* character of *language*" (1996a, 19; my emphasis). This is an extension of the argument encountered in chapter 3. Language as a medium of communication is governed by all sorts of rules involving syntax and semantics. It is incumbent upon individuals to learn and observe those rules if they hope to be members of a human community. "The demand for the recognition of the *objectivity of meaning* is a legitimate one.... If the meanings of symbols [words, etc.] depended on the peculiarities of *individual* minds, inter-personal discourse would be impossible" (Wiredu 1975, 32–33; my emphasis).

If I want to understand and to communicate my understanding to others, assuming I have "normal faculties" and share in "the universality of certain fundamental traits of human beings [reason, reflection, abstraction, etc.]" (Wiredu 1975, 32–33), I must learn the correct way to use language. Wiredu expands upon this in an essay entitled "A Philosophical Perspective on the Concept of Human Communication." There, he further refines the argument involving the rules governing human communication as solid evidence of the *objective subjectivity* of concepts located in the mind: "The basic *biological* similarity of human beings.... A human being is born with a biological make-up, but with no concepts.... To possess a specific concept . . . entails some linguistic ability . . . [which] is the result of training. Human life is a *learning* process. This learning process, which at the start is nothing more than a regime of *conditioning* [by family, society, etc.] is, in fact, the making of *mind*" (Wiredu 1996a, 19; my emphasis).

This builds upon the genetic argument involving *language as rule governed* that was introduced in chapter 3. The question is, Where does it lead? By focusing on communication and what is necessary for it to be successful, Wiredu is able to feature language in a foundational way as governed by rules and principles that provide concepts with syntactical and semantical stability. Nevertheless, the concept of mind itself remains something of a mystery. For Descartes mind still had to be an entity, even if nonmaterial. Must "mind" refer to some kind of *object*, physical or otherwise?

For contrast, Wiredu again turns to the Twi language. What he finds there does not determine his final answer, but it helps him think about the matter in comparative terms. To repeat and expand upon the passage in chapter 3:

In the Akan [Twi] language the word for "thought" is the same as
the word for "mind"; it is *adwene* in both cases. *My own interpretation*
of this and also of Akan usage generally, is that the conception
of "mind" implicit here is of *mind as a function* rather than an
entity. Mind, in this conception, is the *function of thought....*
[Such] linguistic considerations of the sort mentioned ... are not
philosophically decisive. But there are *independent considerations*
for thinking that the conception of mind as a kind of entity is faulty.
(Wiredu 1996a, 16–17; my emphasis in part)[5]

Saying that mind is a function of thought is equivalent to saying mind
is somehow dependent upon or arises out of thought. Given Wiredu's
view of subjectivity, the elements involved are concepts in languages
with meanings—all governed by *rules that make them objective.* This
means that their interconnections are not just surmised. Use of the
word *function* indicates that mind is viewed as an *activity* rather than
an *entity* in its own right:

I hope that it emerges from the foregoing remarks that there is no
real antecedent implausibility in the hypothesis that a *thought* may
be an aspect of a brain state, and *mind* an ongoing complex of such
states. On this hypothesis, be it noted, the mind is not the brain but
rather a certain complicated set of aspects of its states. *Concepts,*
similarly, are no longer conceived of as entities, but aspects of brain
states. Concepts, then, are not in the mind, on the model of items
in a container, but are of the mind; they are the stuff of the mind.
(1996a, 18; my emphasis)

At this point, it should be apparent that how our words refer or relate to the world is of critical importance to Wiredu, Quine, and epistemology generally. Philosophers want to be assured that we are talking
about the world and ourselves in an accurate manner. This therefore
becomes the important consideration for the issue of truth. How are
we to monitor our talk about the world so that we can be assured that

---

5. For those who wish to pursue the matter, he refers them to Wiredu
(1987a), "The Concept of Mind with Particular Reference to the Language
and Thought of the Akans of Ghana."

what we are saying is so? When Wiredu surveys the relevant philosophical literature, he finds that it names three theories that stipulate
how to understand and to measure truth: *correspondence, coherence,*
and *pragmatic theory.* In his analyses, he will amalgamate pragmatic
theory with coherence and end up with only two. In this chapter, he
will evaluate both and end up by endorsing coherence theory as the
more reasonable.

Correspondence theory can seem a product of straightforward common sense because truth is defined as when a statement corresponds to
its object. But more careful consideration of the world of things makes
it difficult to see how a declarative statement such as "The leaves of that
plant are poisonous" is verified directly and simply by a plant. Something more than the plant is needed in order to determine whether
it is true. A better explanation is that our statements are true when
they correspond to the appropriate *facts* about the world. Correspondence theory needs *facts* in order to make sense. "A statement may be
about a tree, but the *fact* which makes it true would not itself be a tree"
(Wiredu 1980c, 154). This requires the existence of a "realm of facts
as an ontological order distinct from the realm of statements and
entities [things] such as trees and houses" (1980c, 154).

English-language academic philosophy that subscribes to this kind
of correspondence theory involving facts has its problems. Wiredu
details three:

1. A declarative statement ("I parked the car behind the house") that
can be empirically verified—the person involved goes out to look—is
thereby proved true. Why is it then necessary to have, in addition,
something called a "fact" that also proves it true (1980c, 157)?

2. The *methodological* procedure stipulated in order to prove a
declarative statement true does not make sense. The recommended
way to proceed is to first formulate the statement and then look for
the relevant fact(s) to confirm it. But this is not the way we proceed.
"A rational man does not first form a belief and then ask for the
evidence in support of it" (1980c, 157). *Evidence,* however it is constituted, plays an essential part in formulating a statement from the
beginning.

3. Once one has affirmed a statement as worth defending, how is one to proceed to determine whether it does in fact correspond to the relevant facts? Does this mean that one should then look for relevant evidence? Surely that is what one has been doing from the beginning. "Clearly, as far as ordinary inquiry is concerned, there is nothing further to do" (Wiredu 1980c, 158). Facts, then, are superfluous.

The cumulative effect of these criticisms is that the Wiredu who, a while back, endorsed the *introduction of facts* only did so with respect to *making sense* of correspondence theory, not epistemology generally. Now he is suggesting that even with the addition of facts, *the correspondence theory does not make sense*.

Wiredu then proceeds to look for evidence of correspondence theory in Twi language usage. That he does not find usage involving or implying correspondence will lead him, once again, to the conclusion that this supposedly *universal* problem of philosophy—*the nature of correspondence*—is not really universal. Here is a summary of that argument:

1. Students of philosophy almost inevitably end up in a course on epistemology. There they encounter something called the correspondence theory of truth, which stipulates that a statement is true when it corresponds to a fact ("in the world"). Philosophers have labored long and hard to make explicit what such correspondence involves.

2. In the Twi language of the Akan people of Ghana, there is no *one word* for "truth." The Akan simply say that *something is so*, an expression that can be used to apply to a *proposition* or *statement*.[6]

3. In the Twi language, there also is no one word equivalent for the English word *fact*. Again, if the Akan want to say that something is the case *about the world*, they use the same expression and say that *something is so*.

---

6. The *Concise Oxford English Dictionary* records this form of usage for the word *so* in the English language as "In that state or condition, actually the case" and cites as one example, "God said 'Let there be light' and it was so" (1964, 1213).

4. The consequence is that the two components of correspondence theory—a *statement* and the *fact* that can make that statement true or false—are not expressed by different words in Twi.

> In Akan [Twi] the [English-language] notions of *truth* and *fact* may be rendered by means of *one notion*, namely, the notion of what is so, *nea ete saa*. The sentence "'p' is true" may be expressed as "'p' *te saa*" and "It is a fact that p" as *Nea ete ne se* p. The expressions *(e)te saa* and *nea ete ne se* are just grammatical variants for rendering the idea of being so. In the upshot, the Akan [Twi] version of the formula amounts, roughly, to saying something like "'p' is so if and only if what is so is that p," which is an unconcealed *tautology.*[7] To be sure, all tautologies are splendid truths. But some are conceptually informative, and others are not; and certainly *this one is not.* From it, therefore, no philosophical enlightenment can be anticipated. . . . *although the equivalence "'p' is true if and only if it is a fact that p" is correct and philosophically interesting in English, it is truistic* [tautologous] *in Akan* [Twi] *but of no philosophical interest."* (Wiredu 2004, 48; my emphasis)

5. Trying to express the point of correspondence theory in Akan (Twi) is a tautology: "'p' is so because 'p' is so."[8] That can also be expressed as "things are as a statement says they are if and only if things are as they are said to be in the statement" (Wiredu 1996g, 108).

6. What's the philosophical significance of this? When students are introduced to epistemology and to correspondence theory via the English language, "truth" and "fact" are treated as two concepts fundamental to human understanding *in all natural languages.*

7. The Twi language demonstrates that equivalents of the terms *statement* and *fact* are *not necessary components of a natural language.*[9]

---

7. The subject and predicate of the statement say the same thing.

8. Wiredu points out that an added complication in going from English to Twi is that the Twi language does not have a phrase corresponding to *equivalence.* Twi can express something like it in a more roundabout (periphrastic) way by saying that two equivalent statements have the same destination, or more literally, "they both reach the same place" (Wiredu 1996g, 109).

9. Quine's IT again becomes relevant.

Therefore, the issue of what properly constitutes *correspondence does not arise.* "From which it follows," says Wiredu, "that some philosophical problems [in this case the nature of correspondence] are not universal" (1996g, 109) to every language culture. That *"some philosophical problems . . . are relative to particular natural languages . . .* [indicates] they *cannot be as fundamental* as *those that are universal to all natural languages"* (1996g, 110; my emphasis).[10]

Use of the term "fundamental" is often a sign that Wiredu is transitioning to a genetic approach. Is that the case here as well? It does seem that being able to say something is true ("'p' is so") is *more fundamental* than any supplementary theory, coherence or correspondence, to explain how that can be the case. As Wiredu puts it, "No cogent thinking is possible without the [fundamental] notion of something being so," and "being so is more fundamental than that of the relation of truth to fact" (Wiredu 1996g, 110). Would it also make sense to say this seems more a consequence of analysis? Or does it win the case that being able to say something is true enables us to cope with our overall environment and is therefore foundational to survival? This is one of those situations where it is left to the reader to decide whether his argumentation is best regarded as analytic, genetic, or both.

Analytic philosophers can be empirically minded when it comes to truth. This has sometimes led to their being labeled as *positivists.* Positivism is an established tradition in philosophy that is identified with those who endorse observation and experience—in effect, empirical experience—as the legitimate source of all knowledge. This was enshrined in what they called the verification principle (of meaning). For a statement to be rated *meaningful,* what it referred to had to be something that could be experienced *empirically* (via the senses) and thereby *verified.* Talk about trees would pass the positivist's test. Talk about spirits, if it is impossible to experience them empirically, would not and therefore be considered meaningless. If philosophers dared to advance original theories that went well beyond empirical experience,

---

10. See discussions of tongue dependency in chapter 3 and later in this chapter.

they were criticized as indulging in *metaphysical speculations* that couldn't be proved true or false and therefore were *meaningless*.

Wiredu addresses this controversy and develops an original approach to the issues of evidence and truth. In doing so, *he will reject positivism* for being too extreme about what it can accept as philosophically legitimate and meaningful. It is therefore ironic that today Wiredu is sometimes, almost pejoratively, labeled a positivist or neopositivist. It can be said that in his writings about the cultures of Africa, Wiredu does emphasize empirical considerations that underlie and involve African beliefs and practices. But this is not evidence of positivism. This is his enduring response to the typing of those cultures as "primitive," a term whose use was conventional in the Department of Anthropology at Oxford University in his student days. Such cultures were said to be less concerned than their modern counterparts with things like empirical evidence, critical thinking, and objective truth. How could the Wiredu who is committed to placing Africa's indigenous cultures on the same intellectual playing field as the rest of the world not respond forcefully to this negative stereotype?

To explain in detail why he does not consider himself a positivist, Wiredu produced a short essay entitled "Brief Remarks on Logical Positivism" (2002a). By combining his statements there with a passage from another important piece published in the same volume, "Kwasi Wiredu: The Making of a Philosopher," in which he details firsthand his intellectual and philosophical development, the following passage is the result:

> Calling me a logical positivist is an interesting mistake. . . . I believe that the positivists did valuable work in logic and the philosophy of science. . . . I do not find, however, that what is of value in their work is peculiar to them or has any logical connection with the verification principle. . . . In my opinion both the logical positivists and their critics were mistaken in regarding this principle as a principle of meaningfulness, whether good or bad. . . . Such was the poverty of logical positivism. (Wiredu 2002a, 321–22; 2002b, 334)[11]

---

11. As will be clear from the next chapter, Wiredu could not agree with this well-known statement with reference to ethics by positivist A. J. Ayer:

As we now know, he very definitely thinks there is much more to the philosophical enterprise than analysis. There are numerous passages in his writings devoted to empirically based speculation arising from his use of analysis and a genetic methodology. This is not positivism. It makes good sense philosophically that there is some empirical relevance to our speculations that can be made available, in principle, to other observers. A genetic approach allows Wiredu to engage with areas and issues that analytic philosophy and positivism would find inappropriate. Should his genetic claims then be regarded as metaphysics, as idle speculations, as far as academic philosophy is concerned? Wiredu does not think so because even if "the *genetic method* in philosophy is as yet undeveloped" (1980c, 165), it has a solid environmental foundation.

With reference to the *coherence theory* of truth, Wiredu aims to convince us that opting for coherence will result in a genetically informed epistemology. To begin with, he sees an overlap between the version of the pragmatic theory of truth advanced by the philosopher John Dewey and coherence theory that makes it possible to combine the two (Wiredu 1980c, 161).[12] The sense of coherence is as follows: In simple terms, let's think of our knowledge as a body of diverse information that we rely upon as and when needed. Then it happens that we are presented with *a new piece of information* that could also qualify as knowledge. In order to do so, it must not contradict or be inconsistent

---

"For in *saying* a certain type of action is right or wrong, I am not making any factual statement, *not even a statement about my own mind*. I am merely expressing certain moral *sentiments* [feelings]. And the man who is ostensibly contradicting me is merely expressing his moral *sentiments*" (Ayer 1936, 159; my emphasis).

12. According to Wiredu, Dewey's version of the pragmatic theory of truth is "An *idea*, that is a hypothetical proposal, is true if it leads to the satisfactory solution of a problem" (Wiredu 1980c, 159). Because the reasonableness endorsed by Wiredu's version of coherence theory stipulates that an idea becomes warrantedly assertible when it either does not cause a problem or solves a problem within an established system of beliefs, that makes his position compatible with Dewey's (Wiredu 1980c, 161; 2007b).

with the knowledge that we already have, which is another way of saying it *must cohere with the body of knowledge we already have.*

Wiredu notes the importance of *noncontradiction* to being able to say a new piece of information is reasonable as therefore worthy of incorporation.[13] If it qualified as *unreasonable*, then it *would not cohere* with the information that previously proved reliable. This is standard coherence theory, but from this point on, he diverges from the traditional version: "To say of a claim that it coheres with a system of knowledge is to say that it is *warrantably assertible*" (Wiredu 1980c, 160) He describes the process of reconciling the new information with the old as *rational investigation.* Via this process of rational investigation, we may also discover that the new information does contradict or put into question a significant portion of the old. If it does, the only way to resolve that problem is via further rational investigation:

> Rational investigation. . . . it is this method which gives *system* [coherence] to the bits of information and deductions which we call our *knowledge.* Moreover, it is only in virtue of this consideration that we can explain *how a new development may lead to large-scale revision* of previously accepted conceptions. Various bits of putative knowledge may fall, but the method itself stands. For this reason, the coherence theory is strictly to be understood as saying, not that *truth* is what coheres with our knowledge—which would be circular in any case, since knowledge involves truth—but rather that which *coheres with our system of beliefs.* (Wiredu 1980c, 161; my emphasis)

"Beliefs" is appropriate because the process of *rational investigation* makes us realize that pieces of information that we label as knowledge (true) can at some point be proved false.[14] In that case, it is more accurate to describe our reliable information as a *system of beliefs* rather than knowledge or a system of knowledge (Wiredu 1980c, 161). That is

---

13. For his earlier discussion of the principle of noncontradiction as well as of genetic origin, see chapter 2.

14. Wiredu once told me he considered himself a humanistic rationalist.

why Wiredu introduces the phrase *warrantably assertible* to describe our reliable information.[15] There is sufficient evidence for the information we adhere to for us to say it is warrantably (justifiably) assertible (maintained). But new information can come along that makes it untrue or incoherent, so it makes better sense to relocate everything to a level of belief.[16]

The consequences for epistemology are significant. Use of the term "belief" rather than "knowledge" indicates that *the degree of certainty assigned to information is conditional*, not absolute. This also makes a genetic approach to our beliefs newly relevant. Our beliefs are expressed via concepts. The analytic approach may enable us to better understand the meanings and interrelations of those concepts. But it does not enable us to know how those concepts came to be in the first place: "there is no reason why the philosopher should remain professionally incurious about the origin of concepts" (Wiredu 1980c, 162).[17]

Early on Wiredu published an essay entitled "Truth as Opinion" (1980e) that attracted interest because it appeared to resurrect Bishop Berkeley's "to be is to be perceived" epistemology. In this essay, Wiredu challenges what he describes as "objectivist" theories of truth that treat their subject matter (truth) as something that is stable and eternal. According to this view, the major problem with "knowledge" as "truth" is for human beings to reach and finally confirm it. For Wiredu that view of the situation is misleading. Discovering truth is in fact *an unending process* in which the beliefs involved are continuously being refined via processes of rational inquiry. "Truth as opinion" is more accurately described as "truth as *considered opinion*," which appears to be an earlier way of phrasing "warranted assertibility."

---

15. The phrase *warrantably assertible* was originally coined by John Dewey, which Wiredu acknowledges.

16. See also Hallen and Sodipo (1997), chapter 2, "An African Epistemology: The Knowledge-Belief Distinction and Yoruba Discourse."

17. "The fundamental features of our conceptual network[s] as an accumulation of developments arising out of the needs of life in its 'transactions' with the environment" (Wiredu 1980c, 170).

If we are serious about the business of understanding how our concepts may have come about, we proceed genetically:

> The empirical approach to the problem of the *origin of concepts* is to attend to basic aspects of life with a view to seeing *how our most fundamental concepts reflect environmentally-determined needs*. Take, for example, the concept "good reason". Is it plausible to suppose that the *genesis* of this concept is completely unrelated to the exigencies of *action*?[18] Human beings must act one way or another to live at all. In action we must depend on all sorts of hypotheses about means and consequences. The good hypothesis is obviously the one that will carry us safely to our destination. (Wiredu 1980c, 164; my emphasis)

To review his overall use of the Twi language in his argumentation, what exactly is the significance of the fact (!) that Twi does not make an explicit distinction between a statement and the fact that can make that statement true or false? What if someone was to reach this point in Wiredu's analysis and say, "Well, this is an African language. Maybe they haven't reached a point in their intellectual development where they appreciate how important it is to make a more explicit distinction between statement and fact"? Wiredu lives in the real world, and given the lack of philosophical respect Africa has been shown in the past, he appreciates there might still be this kind of reaction on the part of some commentators. He reaffirms what is meant to be a clear and reasonable alternative to this kind of thinking.

1. The Twi language demonstrates that *some philosophical problems*—like the nature of correspondence—are *relative* to particular natural languages. The problem arises from English-language usage, but it does not arise from Twi-language usage.

2. If such problems can be *relative* to a particular natural language, they qualify as what Wiredu has described as *tongue-dependent*: "they cannot be as fundamental as those that are *universal* to all natural languages" (Wiredu 1996g, 110). "When the determining factor is language, I have called this dependency tongue-dependency. Of such a

---

18. Rather than trying to be perfectly rational as an end in itself.

nature is the equivalence thesis relating truth to fact, and the language involved is English. Probably, all languages generate some tongue [language] dependent problems and theses. *It therefore behooves every philosopher, whatever his or her language, to watch and pray lest he or she confuse tongue-dependency issues with universal ones*" (Wiredu 2004b, 49; my emphasis).[19]

3. What sorts of *philosophical problems* can be regarded as truly *universal*? He suggests that the idea of *implication* would qualify because "any natural language will have to be capable of expressing this concept in one way or another" (Wiredu 1996g, 110). Any natural language must take into account the distinction between reasons and conclusions, and, more technically, *entailment*, which can be defined in terms of implication.[20] "Such a question [the relation between the premises and conclusion of an argument] would be universal to all natural languages in the sense that it can be posed for any *intuitively workable logic* that may be constructed in any natural language" (1996g, 110; my emphasis). What does Wiredu mean by intuitively workable logic? Is he saying Twi-language usage expresses a logic, involving things like implication and entailment, that is universal? Recalling his view of languages as governed by rules, that is indeed what he is saying: "The hastiness, not to talk of the absurdity, of a rather more alarming idea which frequently lies behind the remark that *logic is non-African*. I refer to the idea that *logical thinking*, not just the construction of systems of logic, is not a characteristic of the African. . . . Presupposed by the logic or philosophy of any discipline is logic in the fundamental sense of the *principles of correct reasoning*. . . . *Logic*, then, in the most fundamental sense, is *presupposed by language*" (Wiredu 1996d, 83–84; my emphasis).

4. If language presupposes logic, then there is no *reason* to deny it to any language culture. "It follows that the problem concerning

---

19. For relevant discussion, see earlier in this chapter.

20. *Implication*: recognizing that it is possible for two statements to be related so that the second is seen as a consequence of the first ("If p then q"). *Entailment*: recognizing what it means for one statement to be the consequence of another statement (the q in "If p then q").

[something's] *being so is more fundamental* [and therefore clearly of genetic origin] than that of *the relation of truth to fact*" (1996g, 110; my emphasis).

5. There remains "a *problem of truth* in the Twi language" (1996g, 110; my emphasis), of what is involved in something's *being so*. According to Wiredu, this does not make it difficult for the Akan to make knowledge claims about the world, but it does make their language less interesting from an epistemological point of view, given the current *priorities* of academic philosophy.

Wiredu's translations and use of the Twi language have not gone unchallenged. His philosophical colleague J. T. Bedu-Addo (1981), another native Twi speaker, argues that Wiredu's personal preference for coherence theory causes him to misrepresent Twi meanings so they will not support correspondence theory.[21] "It would seem, then, that in examining the concept of truth in Akan [Twi], Wiredu relied almost exclusively on the technique of philosophical reflection [his own epistemological preferences], and did not really feel called upon to employ, in addition, the method of actually questioning other competent speakers of Akan, in the good old Socratic manner [i.e., ordinary language]" (Bedu-Addo 1981, 75). Bedu-Addo uses an ordinary language approach supplemented by his own conceptual analyses. He argues there are specific expressions in Twi that can be used to describe a statement as true in its own right, and there are expressions in Twi that can be used to refer to things that are comparable to facts: "As I have tried to show, in Akan the phrase *ete saa (otse dem)* is used not only with reference to statements, but also to things" (1981, 83). In that case, Twi does manifest usage that implies and accommodates correspondence theory.

---

21. Wiredu denies using Twi *language usage to prove* coherence: "When I have taken it into my head to argue in favor of the pragmatic [coherence] or against the correspondence theory, I have done so on independent grounds, that is, on the basis of considerations that do not depend on the peculiarities of Akan [Twi] or any other language" (Wiredu 1996h, 204).

Wiredu has responded to Bedu-Addo's criticisms in several places.[22] In effect, he challenges Bedu-Addo's own translations and analyses of Twi as in fact proving that "both 'truth' and 'fact' [are expressed by] the same notion" (1996h, 209). Arbitration by other knowledgeable translators would be helpful.

A. G. A. Bello, in an article entitled "Philosophy and an African Language," also objects that Wiredu improperly invokes Twi-language usage to validate his eventual rejection of correspondence as an epistemological alternative: "We must be wary of using purely linguistic facts (for example translatability or non-translatability) as knockdown arguments for philosophical beliefs or doctrines" (Bello 1987, 7).[23] It seems this is a challenge that could be raised against his use of the Twi language from the very beginning. If something is the case in the Twi language, does that make it philosophically preferable?

Wiredu, in turn, objects that he has explicitly ruled out *using* the Twi language in this way: "The point [of any philosophical argument] ought, on the appropriate occasion, to be *demonstrable* in the English language itself and *on independent grounds*" (1980a, 35; my emphasis).[24] Bello acknowledges this statement by Wiredu but then charges that he does not practice what he preaches. It may be the case that when the meaning of correspondence—statement correctly represents fact—is translated into Twi, it becomes a tautology and is thereby philosophically trivialized. But this says more about the imperfections of the Twi language than it does about the oddities of English:

> If the correspondence theory is unstatable in the Akan [Twi] language, so much the worse for that language. That, in itself, says nothing about the correspondence theory; nothing about its plausibility or its being fundamental or not. However, it does say

22. "Truth: The Correspondence Theory of Judgment" (1987b, n17), "The Concept of Truth in the Akan Language" (1995, n3), and "Postscript: Reflections on Some Reactions" (1996h, 208–9).

23. Bello also puts it this way: "The language of a people can be a good index or pointer to a people's philosophy, [but] linguistic considerations alone cannot in themselves be decisive in philosophical disputes" (1987, 5).

24. See the quotation in chapter 2.

a lot about the Akan [Twi] language. It means that the language is not suitable for discussing certain theories. It also means that the Akan [Twi]-speaking peoples have to brace up to the fact that their language or conceptual apparatus needs development in this small area in which it does not facilitate clarity and exactness of thought, since it promotes the constant conflation of the meanings of "truth" and "fact," by rendering both as *nea ete sua* (literally, what is "so"). (Bello 1987, 8)

Bello is saying the language has a conceptual problem that should be corrected. In a subsequent publication, Wiredu disagrees with the claim that he says or implies correspondence theory is somehow defective because it cannot be translated into Twi as anything other than a tautology. It is also not the case that theories that can be meaningfully translated into Twi are thereby validated: "When I say that a theory does not suffer trivialization on being translated into Akan [Twi], I do not mean—and I cannot be rightly interpreted to mean—that it is therefore any better than one which suffers trivialization. It may not suffer that fate [trivialization] and yet be egregiously absurd [ridiculous content] in Akan [Twi] discourse, and outside it too" (1996h, 203).

Finally, there is another reason he believes it appropriate to involve African vernaculars with academic philosophy: "I do recommend that wherever possible African philosophers should take cognizance, in their philosophical meditations, of the intimations of their own languages. . . . because of the historical fact of colonialism, which led not only to the relative neglect of our *indigenous philosophies* in our own thinking but also to the distortions of our conceptual frameworks through their articulation in the medium of *foreign categories of thought*" (1996h, 208; my emphasis). As he has suggested, some of the problems that academic philosophy currently treats as universal are consequences of the grammar and vocabulary of specific natural languages, such as English. That is why he describes them as tongue (language) dependent. The grammars and vocabularies of other natural languages, such as Twi, may not invite those problems and offer coherent alternatives that elevate reflective understanding. In that case, Twi does not have to be seen as somehow defective for not clearly articulating different concepts comparable to truth and fact. Twi usage can even be seen in a positive light as philosophically suggestive, insofar as it could be said to support the identity of truth and fact. This makes it consistent with philosopher P. F. Strawson's claim (1978, 293) of such equivalence, "Facts are what statements (when true) state," or with philosopher Peter Herbst's (1963, 134) definition of fact as "what is stated by a true statement."

Wiredu's views of ontology segued into his philosophy of language. His philosophy of language informs his epistemology and theory of truth. The two remaining chapters will concern his views relating to *ethics* and to *social and political* philosophy. It will be of special interest to see whether these areas are also open to a genetic approach.

FIVE

On Sympathetic Impartiality

IN HIS QUINE CRITIQUES, WIREDU first analyzes that philosopher's argumentation and then goes a step further by undertaking a genetic inquiry to identify ultimately environmental considerations that may have influenced Quine's philosophical thinking. When it comes to *ethics*, Wiredu's genetic methodology, as practiced, is somewhat different. For one thing, he does not have Quine as an adversary. For another, the methodological perspective he first explicitly endorses is *naturalism*, even if it is almost immediately linked to a genetic approach.[1] To repeat the passage quoted in chapter 3: "The mention of the term 'naturalistic' brings us to an important type of philosophical outlook which may be regarded as the genus of which the genetic approach is a species. 'Naturalism' in philosophy is a broad rubric covering every manner of philosophizing in which explanations and elucidations are developed exclusively in terms of *factors relating to man and external nature.* Thus, obviously, genetic epistemology is naturalistic" (Wiredu 1980c, 171; my emphasis). In that case, adopting a genetic method is, in effect, using a naturalistic approach. But genetic *epistemology* is not genetic *ethics*. It is best, then, to proceed on a tentative basis, to see whether his strategy is to arrive at underlying or foundational factors in the domain of ethics.

---

1. See also the earlier discussion of naturalism in chapter 3.

Wiredu tells us that we must tread carefully when arguing about ethics or morality. These are areas of philosophy that can be problematically personal: "The religious, moral and social areas of philosophy are the areas in philosophy which impinge most directly on feelings, emotions and aspirations; they are consequently the areas in which prejudices are most likely to impede the course of objective reflection (Wiredu 1980c, 172). Because of this, students of philosophy had best begin their training with the "comparatively unemotional subjects of logic and epistemology," where an emphasis on the quality of argument and evidence is undisputed (1980c, 172). That also happens to be the way the chapters in this text are organized, but that has been done because of the priority assigned to identifying Wiredu's methodology rather than considerations relating to pedagogy.

Prejudices can be ethnocentric as well as personal, as the case of Africa demonstrates. The supposedly exotic, bizarre, and less than optimal character of African morality has been stereotyped by too many sources. Wiredu's objective is to reintroduce ethical and moral Africa to academic philosophy by identifying the ethical universals that are shared with the rest of the world, and to do this using an expository tone and argumentation that avoids any form of emotional appeal.

Over the years, Wiredu has published a number of essays that detail the ethical and moral beliefs and practices of his native Akan culture.[2] In them, he sometimes provides accounts that are so detailed as to be ethnographic in character and so are not directly relevant to the priorities of the present text. But he also arrives at generalizations about Akan and African cultures that are relevant. Here is a synopsis of some of that argumentation.

"Community" in the African sense involves much more than the Western notion of a "body of people living in the same locality" (*Concise Oxford English Dictionary* 1964, 245). In Africa, generally "a person is social not only because he or she lives in a community . . . but also because, by his original constitution, *a human being is part of a social whole*" (Wiredu 1998b, 309; my emphasis). One wants more specifics as to what this actually involves. Wiredu is willing to go into greater

---

2. As evidenced by the contents of Wiredu and Gyekye (1992).

detail as long as he can source his own Akan culture, which he believes to be generally representative of sub-Saharan Africa.

1. The sense of *community* in the Akan culture is linked to a particular view of morality. Being moral in a communal setting is what transforms a human being into an authentic *person*. Being a person "means that an individual's image will depend rather crucially upon the extent to which his or her *actions benefit others than himself . . . by design. . . .* an individual who remained content with self-regarding successes would be viewed as so circumscribed in outlook as *not to merit the title of a real person*" (1998b, 312; my emphasis). Becoming and being recognized as a person, rather than merely human, involves a *moral* dimension as importantly as a social one.

2. *Family* in the African context is what is sometimes referred to as the extended family. Whether defined by the male or female line, family may encompass one's grandfather or grandmother and all his or her children and grandchildren, as well as the grandfather's or grandmother's brothers and sisters and their children and grandchildren. This is not to say that all these people live in the same household, but these are the people who constitute one's immediate relations and kin, and who constitute basic components of an individual's moral upbringing. "For the dissemination of moral education or the reinforcement of the will to virtue. . . . the theater of moral upbringing is the home, at parents' feet and within range of kinsmen's inputs. The mechanism is precept, example and correction. The temporal span of the process is lifelong, for, although upbringing belongs to the beginning of our earthly careers, the need for correction is an unending contingency in the lives of mortals" (Wiredu 1998b, 308).

3. Two other moral considerations relevant to achieving *personhood* are as follows:

   a. *Morality* is not regarded as a purely intellectual or rational undertaking. Passions and feelings may be involved in any moral conflict, and therefore *goodwill* as well as duty are involved. This is something Wiredu specifically remarks on as generally true of African societies. By goodwill, he means some form of "human sympathy" or

"sentimentality" that goes beyond mere duty, or of goodwill as merely a function of duty (Wiredu 1998b, 310). As
he puts it, "There will always be something unlovable
about correctness of conduct bereft of passion. . . . the
ultimate moral inadequacy consists in that lack of feeling which is the root of selfishness" (1998b, 310).

b. *Personhood*—being recognized as a morally enlightened
and responsible member of the community—is the ultimate moral accolade. But this would never be attributed
to an individual whose motives were primarily self-
interested. Relationships with and responsibilities to kith
and kin are meant to make moral isolation difficult. This
means that some everyday actions are deliberately meant
to better others rather than oneself. Indeed, the typical
Akan is conscious of and scrupulous to protect his or her
personhood status throughout his or her lifetime.

4. For Wiredu, the basis of the quest for personhood in Akan moral
thought is social rather than religious. *Morality* in the African communal setting is therefore primarily *humanistic* in character. "One important implication of the founding of value on human interests is the
independence of *morality* from *religion* in the Akan outlook: What is good
in general is *what promotes human interests.* . . . Thus, the will of God, not
to talk of any other extra-human being, is logically incapable of defining
the good" (Wiredu 1998b, 307; my emphasis). Religion or the super-
natural is not foundational to Akan morality. What can be described as
a form of humanism defines the moral as "the basic *naturalistic* thesis
[is] that the concepts and principles of morality derive their whole
meaning from the *nature and needs* of man as a social being" (Wiredu
1980c, 171; my emphasis). Human welfare is the pathway to follow in
order to understand the moral in the African context. The introduction
of naturalism to characterize what promotes human interests in social
environments suggests a *genetic* dimension is being introduced into his
inquiry.

Comparisons of African and Western societies and their values
generally emphasize the aforementioned *communal* character of

Africa. That is frequently contrasted with what is said to be the *individualism* characteristic of Western societies:

> The key [separation] ... is that between the individual and the community: it is the ground of all the other divisions in the society. The most essential embodiment of this phenomenon is the preservation of a zone of individual expression from which community or communal demands are excluded.... the predominant relationship ... is one of mutual indifference among atomistic individuals—sovereigns whose individual zones are sacrosanct and for whom community is inessential—that make it up. (Taiwo 1996, 186)

The communal character of Africa's cultures is often used to set them apart, to capture what is supposedly distinctive about them. The challenge Wiredu faces, using his genetic approach, is to identify something that is foundational to African and Western societies—in fact to all human societies—that still allows them to be characterized as individualistic or communal.

As was the case with the subjective-objective dichotomy in chapter 4, Wiredu begins by suggesting the differences between the communalistic and the individualistic are exaggerated. According to Wiredu, "the real difference between communalism and individualism has to do with *custom* and *lifestyle* rather than anything else.... both are, conceptually, of a kind and are *distinct from morality in the strict sense*" (1996i, 72; my emphasis).

When observing their own or alien cultures, people generally and scholars frequently focus on what Wiredu describes as customs and lifestyles. He acknowledges that we cannot make sense of any society unless we take them into account. They are of instrumental and empirical value for highlighting the diversity of ways in which human beings invent themselves. But they are also comparatively superficial. Wiredu suggests that people who emphasize the relativity of *moral values* between cultures place undue emphasis on contingent differences in customs and lifestyles rather than *foundational moral principles*. He therefore relegates *customs* to the status of "*contingent* norms[3] of life

---

3. Which is defined as "standard, pattern, type" (*Concise Oxford English Dictionary* 1964, 820).

rather than forms of morality in the strict sense of the word" (1996b, 30; my emphasis) and argues that they can include "*usages, traditions, manners, conventions, grammars, vocabularies, etiquette, fashions, aesthetic standards, observances, taboos, rituals, folkways, [and] mores*" (1996b, 28; my emphasis).[4]

He spends less time detailing *lifestyle*, saying only that it is "more readily associated with how each *individual* chooses to live" (1996i, 72; my emphasis) and is, for example, evidenced by certain elements of stoicism and Epicureanism that are even more morally superficial than customs (1996b, 30). In dictionary searches, it was difficult to find a definition of *lifestyle*, apart from circular attempts along the lines of "the style of life adopted by a person or group that reflects their values." If he means lifestyle to be more individualistic, then presumably vegetarians may be said to have adopted a certain lifestyle insofar as it affects their diet. Nomads may be said to have a certain lifestyle insofar as it affects their movements. Priests may be said to have adopted a certain lifestyle insofar as it affects their personal life. To complicate matters, presumably the same individual could be a vegetarian, nomad, and priest.

If being communal or individualistic, as well as customs and lifestyles, are all comparatively *superficial* attributes, does this mean there is some more *foundational moral principle* at work in human societies? The answer is yes. To illustrate his now naturalistic and genetic approach to morality as it occurs in any society, Wiredu introduces a *universal* principle that all human beings must live by if any community or society is to survive. He describes it as the *principle of sympathetic impartiality*. "What of the *biologic* basis of ethical norms? . . . The need for morality arises from facts of the following kind. Human beings have common as well as conflicting interests. Coexistence in a society requires some adjustment or reconciliation of these interests. The possibility of such an adjustment rests on the fact that human beings do have a basic *natural sympathy* for their kind" (1996o, 41).

---

4. Grammars and vocabularies are reminiscent of syntax and semantics as mentioned in chapter 2.

Morality, from the standpoint of conduct, is the *motivated pursuit of sympathetic impartiality.* Such values as truthfulness, honesty, justice, chastity, etc. are simply aspects of sympathetic impartiality, and do not differentiate morality from culture to culture. At best, what the contingencies of culture may do is to introduce variations of detail in the definition of some of these values. (1996b, 30; my emphasis).

Wiredu doesn't mean for the principle to be prescriptive. It is genetic, a consequence of humanity's involvement with the environments—natural and social—with which it must come to terms: "It seems clear, in any case, whether or not, as a matter of philosophy, people take *this principle to be the basis of all morals* that, as a *fact* [!] *of ethical life,* it is essential to the harmonization of human interests in society" (1996b, 29; my emphasis). It is important to remember that humanity itself constitutes one of those environments—how we get on with one another. The principal argument in support of the principle is that it *promotes human welfare* in *any environment.* This is supported in a variety of ways: "I suggest that it takes little imagination to foresee that life in any society in which everyone openly avowed the contrary of this principle and acted accordingly would inevitably be 'solitary, poor, nasty, *brutish,*' and probably short" (1996b, 29). "My argument is that *morality is a universal* because it is necessary for the *existence* of a human community" (1996h, 202; my emphasis). "I have suggested what might be called irreversibility in principle as the hallmark of pure morality and have suggested a thought experiment for detecting it (hopefully!)" (2008, 336).

Irreversibility and thought experiment presumably refer to the indispensable status of the principle. In its absence, no enduring human society is feasible. "What we need to do is to specify a principle of conduct such that *without its recognition*—which does not necessarily mean its invariable observance—*the survival of human society in a tolerable condition* would be inconceivable" (1996b, 29; my emphasis).[5] "Let your conduct at all times manifest a due concern for the interests

---

5. Invariable observance is relevant to the issue of environmental determinism in chapter 6. As for survival, "It is true that individuals and

of others. . . . A person may be said to manifest due concern for the interests of others if in contemplating the impact of his actions on their interests, she puts herself imaginatively in their position, and having done so, is able to welcome that impact" (1996b, 29).

Wiredu acknowledges the principle is comparable to the Golden Rule's "Do unto others as you would have others do unto you." The difference is that Wiredu's principle is *essential*, a sine qua non, to the overall existence of human society, whereas the Golden Rule is often presented as a kind of *ideal* left for humanity to embrace. He also acknowledges that the principle is comparable to Kant's categorical imperative: "Act only according to that maxim whereby you can, at the same time, will that it should become a universal law."[6] But Kant's version is the product of a strict rationalist tradition that becomes an aberration when thinking in international or cross-cultural terms. A genuine *humanism*, such as that engendered by the principle of sympathetic impartiality, finds Kant's divide between the rational and the emotional unacceptable for formulating a basis for moral values and moral acts. Wiredu finds duty in the deontologically pure Kantian sense, as expressed by an exclusively or purely *rational* sense, to be neither a sufficient nor satisfactory basis for *humanism*.[7] Kant's categorical imperative needs to be improved with "a dose of compassion" so that feeling and emotion—sentiment—and *goodwill* are not left out and treated as somehow irrelevant to morality (Wiredu 1996b, 29).

Wiredu makes the principle sympathetic to highlight the element of *compassion* that is and must be a component of the moral. "We have *not encountered any difference of morality in the strict sense between Akan [and, by extension, African] and Western ways of life*. This is not accidental. If the concern of morality is the harmonization of the interests of the individual with the interests of society, this is exactly what is to

---

groups may differ in their degree of inclination or dedication to such aims, but this is a fact of practice, not of precept" (Wiredu 1996i, 74).

6. Maxim is defined as "Generally any simple and memorable rule or guide for living" (*Oxford Dictionary of Philosophy*, 226). The expression "an eye for an eye" would qualify as a maxim.

7. It is relevant here to recall Wiredu's characterization of himself as a humanistic rationalist.

be expected, for none but the most brutish form of existence could be foreseen among any group of individuals who standardly disavowed and disregarded any such concerns" (1996i, 74; my emphasis). Wiredu appears to have taken something from the notion of the *communal* that is supposedly definitive of African culture and transformed its sense of being concerned for the welfare of others into a universal moral principle whose observance becomes essential to the welfare of any human community.

To reconsider, if the principle of sympathetic impartiality is "a human universal transcending cultures" (1996b, 29), how does one reconcile its universal status with the moral differences found in societies that are still said to evidence, for example, an individualistic rather than a communal orientation? To answer this question, Wiredu asks us to imagine there is a *moral tool* available that amounts to a kind of *sliding scale*. At one end of this scale, we place communities that are said to be decidedly communal in nature, and at the other end, we place those that are said to be decidedly individualistic in character. The scale does not allow for 100 percent communal or individualistic societies. Extremely communal societies must allow for some degree of individuality, and societies that are extremely individualistic must allow for some degree of communality. However, using this tool, the mixture of or the ratio between the two for any society can be measured by sliding the cursor to the appropriate point on the scale. "The distinction between ... [communalism] and individualism is one of degree only; for a considerable value may be attached to communality in individualistic societies just as individuality is not necessarily trivialized within ... [communal societies]" (1996b, 29).

This does not mean that two societies that happen to be measured as equal in terms of their communal and individualistic characters would be identical. But the differences that distinguish them and that might strike the uninformed observer as significant are the relatively superficial things that have been characterized as customs and lifestyles. They can be of ethnographic interest for highlighting the diversity of ways in which the universal moral principle of sympathetic impartiality is complemented in apparently different cultures. But

Wiredu continues to insist that customs and lifestyles "are distinct from morality in the strict sense" (1996i, 72).

This would mean that people who exaggerate the differences between moral values in different cultures are mistakenly exaggerating the relatively superficial anomalies generated by their differences in customs and lifestyles. He therefore continues to describe customs as "contingent norms of life" that can include, to repeat, "usages, traditions, manners, conventions, grammars, vocabularies, etiquette, fashions, aesthetic standards, observances, taboos, rituals, folkways, [and] mores."[8] Customs and lifestyles are therefore primarily of instrumental and empirical interest for highlighting the diversity of ways in which the universal moral principle is supplemented in different cultures and communities.

Given the gradations allowed by the sliding scale, one might think Wiredu would say that the influence of the principle of sympathetic impartiality increases as societies become more communal in character and decreases as societies become more individualistic in character. But that would not seem to be the case. The principle of sympathetic impartiality is a constant that applies at any point along the scale. A society that did not endorse it would not endure. Where Wiredu's argument does lead is that *the moral values supposedly foundational to African societies have been misrepresented.* Obvious and easily observable differences in customs and lifestyles were given a moral status far in excess of what they deserved. (He might say the same for the model of individualistic societies.) To conclude, "Aside from the difference in the manner of viewing the adjustment of interests required by morality, *the real difference between communalism and individualism has to do with custom and lifestyle rather than anything else*" (1996i, 72; my emphasis).

Over the course of his career, Wiredu has consistently argued against those who portray the African *intellect* and the *cultures* it informs as qualitatively *unique.* In fact, the African intellect has always reasoned in a manner that is comparable to rational thought

---

8. Social anthropologists might disagree, but Wiredu would suggest they too have exaggerated the importance of differences in customs and lifestyles.

anywhere. He introduces us to these African ideas and practices about community, the family, and the person so that we can relate to the population of Africa as part of us rather than as the other. The principle of sympathetic impartiality is essential to this as something by which all human beings are formed. This is another step in his campaign to reorient comparative philosophy and cross-cultural studies where Africa is concerned so that everyone is on the same level playing field. No one is so different as to inhabit a different universe. No one is so different as to be essentially superior or inferior on the basis of that difference. Wiredu is committed to a philosophy whereby *all of humanity shares certain universals of genetic origin* that encompass language, truth, and morality. How those things are evidenced in a particular culture should be assigned a high priority for those committed, as he certainly is, to a vision of humanity and philosophy that truly crosses cultures.

In the next chapter, Wiredu will take on the old stereotype of the African tribe and its authoritarian chief. His corrected *re*presentation will highlight the role of consensus in the African context.

~~~

SIX

On Consensus

CONSENSUS HAS BEEN IDENTIFIED BY African philosophers as an element essential to their societies, past and present, that is not assigned the importance it deserves.[1] A legitimate concern, therefore, is why this element supposedly foundational to sub-Saharan African societies came to be underrated.

There are several general notions of consensus that occur in studies related to sub-Saharan African cultures and societies that deserve preliminary consideration. In the discipline of sociology as it relates to Africa, there is considerable discussion of consensus theory. *Consensus theory* is one of those basic sociological frameworks meant to help us analyze and understand human societies generally. Though the theory may be of Western provenance, it is said to be applicable, in principle, to any society in the world. Consensus theory suggests that for a number of human beings to live together, they must agree about certain basic ideas, norms, values, rules, and regulations (Scott and Marshall 2005, 117).

It is also said that the knowledge and endorsement of these ideas, norms, and values is initially imparted to individuals by the family environments in which they are raised. What, more specifically, those

---

1. Some early and prominent figures associated with consensus are Kenneth Kaunda (Zambia), Julius Nyerere (Tanzania), and K. A. Busia (Ghana).

ideas, norms, and values have to be is not specified, which perhaps is acknowledgment of their possible diversity. The ongoing overall consensus that enables such societies to endure is said to arise from the individual choices and intentions of their members. Expositions of consensus theory like to compare the various institutions of a society—the economy, the military, the judicial, and so forth—to the different organs of a human body, with each making its positive contributions to the maintenance, health, and stability of the whole. Consensus theory can accommodate a degree of social conflict and change, but as channeled by the beliefs, practices, and institutions meant to prevent such things from disrupting the overall stability of a society.

Consensus theory is frequently paired with conflict theory, which is said to be its theoretical opposite. *Conflict theory* argues that consensus theory is misguided in that societies are most importantly grounded on competing groups or classes that promote their interests by contesting for control of the institutions of a society (Scott and Marshall 2005, 114). It therefore disputes the exaggerated importance of some overall uniform consensus shared by the individual members of a society. Groups that do succeed in controlling a society's institutions—for example, the economy or the military—will use that power to advance their own interests at the expense of others. Both of these frameworks have been applied by sociologists to the contemporary societies of sub-Saharan Africa. Case in point: Margaret Peil's *Consensus and Conflict in African Societies* (1977), which applies the theories to many different aspects of the societies of 1970s sub-Saharan Africa.

If consensus theory is meant to be applicable, in principle, to any society at any point in its history, what about the case of precolonial Africa? Some accounts of governance there do not seem to support the role of an individual's voluntary consensus with respect to governance:

> In terms of *governance*, tribal society was *undemocratic*. . . . Power and law emanated from the tribal head who governed by divine right rather than the law, mainly because the head was lauded as the representative and spokesperson of the gods as well as the ancestors on earth. Members of the political community could not claim to be independent, autonomous and rational persons with the

right to participate in the governance of a community. They were subservient to the king or chief who embodied the power of the community in himself and exercised it for and on behalf his people. Tribal heads ruled virtually by divine right; and so members of tribal societies had no public space for participation in government. They were subjects, not citizens. (Ninsin 2012, 1118; my emphasis)

If the notion of consensus in consensus theory is meant to involve something voluntary on the part of the population that subscribes to it, such tribal societies so constituted would appear to fall outside of its purview. Consent in this representation of tribal society is demanded of or enforced upon the population by a higher power. Those who dare to disagree or resist may be subject to arbitrarily punitive measures.

To introduce yet another application of the term to the cultures of sub-Saharan Africa, social anthropologist Robin Horton (1993) finds the idea of the consensual appropriate for characterizing what he calls theoretical or abstract thinking in tribal societies in the traditional African cultural context. Analogous to scientific theory, in such cultures various indigenous beliefs and practices (e.g., religion) qualify as theoretical because they are used for the explanation, prediction, and control of events in the world. These beliefs and the practices associated with them in such societies are best described specifically as *traditions* because they are not easily subject to challenge or change. According to Horton, this kind of understanding can therefore be described as *consensual* because a society's members are conditioned to endorse it as is.

Wiredu defends a notion of the African intellect and persona that is diametrically opposed to that associated with the authoritarian chief or the idea of unchanging beliefs and practices.[2] His view of *precolonial* and *postcolonial* African societies is that they were and are grounded on the independent thinking and the individual agency of their members, qualities that were and are fundamental to and definitive of them. Elaborating and commenting on his revisionist view of indigenous African societies therefore becomes a priority. But even at this initial stage, it seems clear that very *different* meanings

---

2. Wiredu once told me that Horton's writings on Africa's cultures had no influence on his own ideas.

of consensus have been used to characterize Africa's societies and cultures.

As was the case with morality, Wiredu's exposition of consensus in the indigenous African context begins with the nature of *community*. The idea of the tribe may have evoked a certain image of community. But tribal governance, as described in the quote above, was mistakenly stereotyped as that of a passive population subordinate to a chief whose authority was absolute. According to Wiredu, being a member of an African community, in precolonial times or today, did not mean that one was part of an authoritarian organic whole in which behavior and thought were regimented. Consensus was always a priority, arising from *intentional, negotiated, rational exchanges* that were a conventional part of everyday life.

This alternative view of the nature of community in the African context generally is termed *communitarianism*. In his writings, Wiredu makes an even finer distinction between communitarianism and what he refers to as *communalism*. By communalism, he means the kind of social order typical of Africa in precolonial times. By communitarianism, he references a social and political philosophy that encompasses carryovers from precolonial times as well as an agenda for today. Wiredu grounds his discussions of communitarianism on hard data derived from firsthand experience of his native Akan culture as well as published historical sources. On that basis, he will endorse a social and political order—*consensual governance*—that he believes, in point of fact and principle, is better suited to the nation-states of sub-Saharan Africa than the so-called liberal democratic forms of government they were persuaded to adopt at the time of independence. What is noteworthy is that he thinks this model for governance can also benefit present-day Western liberal democracies.

There is a significant carryover of content between this chapter on governance and the previous chapter on ethics and morality. As Wiredu notes, "*Ethics*, moreover, may quite naturally be considered as a *preliminary* to political or, more broadly, *social philosophy*, which is concerned with the fundamental problems of the *social institutionalization of the concept of the good*. Social philosophy is, indeed, the crown of all philosophy" (1980c, 172; my emphasis). If the good is defined by the *principle of sympathetic impartiality*, is his aim now to identify the form of political order most compatible with it?

It appears Wiredu first remarked on consensus as a potential *political* plus in a 1977 address to the Ghana Academy of Arts and Sciences.[3]

> A much commended trait of our traditional culture is its infinite capacity for the pursuit of consensus and reconciliation. An urgent task facing us today is to find ways of translating this virtue into institutional forms in our national life. In view of the changes and chances of our recent past [e.g., European colonialism], this is a task to which all of us should address ourselves. *Our culture may yet save us.* (Gyekye 1995, 41–42)

He does not begin to develop the political dimension of consensus in a systematic manner until later on in his writings, in a series of essays articulating what has become known as *consensual democracy*.[4] He begins by telling us that "decision-making in traditional African life and governance was, as a rule, by consensus" (1996j, 182). The phrasing "in traditional African life" is significant because Wiredu wants to claim that "reliance on consensus [in the African context] is *not a peculiarly political phenomenon*. Where consensus characterizes political decision-making in Africa it is a manifestation of *an immanent approach to social interaction*. Generally, in interpersonal relations between adults, consensus as a basis of joint action was taken as axiomatic" (1996j, 182; my emphasis). Does this suggest influence of the *principle of sympathetic impartiality*? "Harking back to my own background of indigenous thought . . . *traditional Akan ethical maxims*, quite demonstrably converge on some such foundation as the *principle of sympathetic impartiality*" (1996b, 29; my emphasis).

Sympathetic impartiality is supposed to be universal. If consensus is not also awarded *universal* status, should it be relegated to the level

---

3. A revised version of the address, which does not contain the passage quoted by Gyekye, is entitled "Philosophy and an African Culture" and can be found at Wiredu (1980d).

4. Wiredu 1996j; 1996k; 1996l; 1996m; 1998a; 1999; 2001a; 2001b; 2007a; 2008; 2012.

of custom? But in Wiredu's view, customs are culturally relative and are not morality in the strict sense. Yet interpersonal relationships in African societies are said to have always generally—on any level—prioritized consensus. Substantive dialogue between divergent individuals in a family or parties in a community enables everyone who is contending "to feel that adequate account has been taken of their points of view" and serves to promote "a willing suspension of disagreement, making possible agreed actions without necessarily agreed notions" (1996j, 183).

This rather complex turn of phrase means that to arrive at a consensus with regard to a specific idea or a specific course of action, other more general beliefs of the contending individuals or parties do not have to change. All those involved have to do is endorse some more specific form of *compromise* to resolve the situation. Reaching a compromise means that different views have influenced and informed it. That one "suspends disagreement" with the outcome when one's views have not completely won out enables a final resolution to be reached. "In a consensus system the voluntary acquiescence of the minority with respect to a given issue would normally be necessary for the adoption of a decision" (1996j, 190).

Wiredu's strategy is to extrapolate the model of consensual governance from his native Akan culture and then promote it as a model for governance of the modern African nation-state. He also sees it as an alternative for Western liberal democracies because it would facilitate more effective participation by citizens in governance. In fact, a form of consensual democracy has also become a topic of interest in contemporary Western liberal democratic theory (Lijphart 2012), where it is said to offer an improvement that would give electorates a more direct role in social and political decision-making processes.

By means of this argument, which is empirically grounded, Wiredu is discarding the model of tribal society as organic and of tribal governance as authoritarian. Whether centralized with a king or chief or decentralized with limited formal governmental structure, *African societies functioned on the basis of consensus*. Kings and chiefs or nomads did not live or govern in splendid isolation. They lived and governed on the basis of consultation and compromise.

My argument will be that consensual governance in our tradition was essentially democratic; that *the majoritarian form of democracy seen in the multiparty systems in Britain and the USA is drastically antithetic to both our own traditions of democracy* and the complexities of our contemporary situation and that, although the kinship basis of our political systems of old cannot be re-invoked in this day and age, it is still a practical proposition to try to fashion out a contemporary *non-party form of government* based on the *principle of consensus.* In this way perhaps we can hope to restore the lost continuity between the state and civil society in Africa. (2012, 1058; my emphasis)

Much of the literature related to the governance of contemporary African nation-states takes the *liberal democratic model* for granted. But in defense of consensual democracy, Wiredu argues that the efforts to install liberal democracies in African countries have been unsuccessful. That is because that model of government does not fit the indigenous consensual social and moral dispositions of African societies, and the resulting incompatibility is largely responsible for the failings and failures of African nation-states—for the corruption, the recurrent ethnic animosities, and the ineffectiveness or eventual collapse of central governments.

In practice, liberal democracy does not promote or sustain continuous participation in governance on the part of the individual citizen. This is an important point. Wiredu will suggest that *participation* on the part of the populace has become a problem for the liberal democracies of the West as well. That is one reason consensus democracy should be considered a positive alternative for them.[5] Liberal democracy advocates events called elections, which happen very occasionally. But those are the only occasions when citizens can exercise what is referred to as their *vote.*[6] Liberal democracy,

---

5. "But there is nothing peculiarly African about the idea [consensual governance] itself. If it is valid, especially with respect to its human rights dimension, *it ought to be a concern for our whole species*" (Wiredu 1996j, 190; my emphasis).

6. "There is no longstanding word for voting in the language of the Ashantis. The expression which is currently used for that process (*aba to*)

in practice, also encourages the formation of *political parties* that contest for overall control of government.

In African countries, which are often composed of a multiplicity of ethnic groups, the different political parties become identified with specific ethnic groups. Because those parties then contest for control of the state, this exacerbates ethnic rivalries and unrest. The liberal democratic model is also identified with the *principle of majority rule*. But this "winner take all" attitude implicitly tends to disenfranchise minorities from playing a significant role in the governing process. "Any element of majoritarianism is a loss of *consensus*" (Wiredu 2012, 1065).

Wiredu asks for help from colleagues in working out the mechanics of consensual governance for the modern nation-state: "At this historical juncture, there is an urgent need for African intellectuals, including historians, philosophers, political scientists, economists, anthropologists, sociologists, linguists, constitutional scholars, jurists, journalists and other leaders of opinion, to put their heads together to explore the history, rationale, conceptual basis and constitutional framework for a non-party system of politics based on consensus" (2012, 1065). He himself has endeavored to expand upon the ramifications of consensus in numerous published essays that are meant to provide some general guidelines.

"The polity we have in mind . . . is completely party-less and motivated by a quite radical commitment to consensus" (Wiredu 2012, 1064). In a consensual democracy, there will be *no political parties*. This means candidates will not run for office on the basis of their party affiliations. As individuals, they will run for office on the basis of their *qualifications* for office: "A less unwelcome use of majorities might occur in the [initial] election of representatives. Here choice may have to be determined by superior numbers in terms of votes. But even here the representatives will be under obligation to consult with all the tendencies of opinions in their constituencies and work out, as much as possible, a consensual basis of representation" (Wiredu 1996j, 190).

---

is an obvious modern coinage for a modern cultural import or, shall we say, imposition" (Wiredu 1996j, 184).

Initially elected (selected?) representatives would not participate in something like town hall meetings where they are there to listen passively to the people they represent. They will have highly motivated meetings with constituents where all participate in discussions about diverse ideas relevant to a particular issue and thereby arrive at a consensus that they can then carry with them to the next level of government. Once at that level of government,

> consensus as a political decision-making procedure requires in principle that each representative should be persuaded, if not of the optimality of each decision, at least of its practical necessity, all things considered. If discussion has been even *moderately rational* and the spirit has been one of *respectful accommodation* on all sides, surviving reservations on the part of a momentary minority will not prevent the recognition that, if the community is to go forward, a particular line of action must be taken .... without the constraints of membership in parties relentlessly dedicated to wresting power or retaining it, representatives will be more likely to be actuated by the *objective merits* of given proposals than by ulterior considerations. In such an environment willingness to compromise, and with it the prospect of consensus, will be enhanced. (Wiredu 1996j, 189–90; my emphasis)

Wiredu has his critics. Some colleagues in African philosophy find his claims of an African heritage of consensus weak on empirical grounds. "The concepts of unanimity, community, solidarity, consensus and the like, through which African societies have been theorized by African writers, are thoroughly mythological, in that they project into a pre-colonial past an Africa without history, without fissures or conflicts, eternalised in a blissful social harmony" (Jacques 2012).[7]

---

7. This criticism is then compromised: "Wiredu's thesis should therefore be evaluated against historical evidence. But a labour of this kind would go beyond the competence of this author, and I accordingly leave it to others" (Jacques 2012, 1024). See Lauer (2012b) for more incisive criticism of his argument. Other African philosophers argue that the east African and south African *ubuntu* vision of humanity also is more compatible with consensual democracy: "*ubuntu* political philosophy would prefer selective consensual

Although critics may question the historical status of consensus, in the absence of empirical evidence to support their own position, they are not able to disprove it—they can only challenge it. An important consideration becomes, How much evidence is there in the literature in support of something like consensus in indigenous African societies? Some measure of reassurance can be gained from the importance accorded another term that seems to qualify as a synonym for consensus, the Portuguese-derived *palaver*.

Even if its meaning has been somewhat abused over the course of time, in sociological and anthropological monographs, *palaver* is used to describe traditional *exercises promoting consensus* in the cultures of Ethiopia, Kenya, Tanzania, and the Democratic Republic of the Congo (UNESCO 1979).[8] In these places, it "has the positive sense of organized and open debates on various issues in which everybody, regardless of age or sex, is encouraged to participate, with a view to reaching *consensus* and keeping the community closely linked" (UNESCO 1979, "Preface"). One of these sources notes that "in regard to the term 'palaver,' it might be interesting to add that a relatively wide review of literature on African *social and political organizations* revealed that *palaver had not hitherto been utilized* either as an analytical or conceptual tool in these areas" (Karanja-Diejomaoh 1979, 44; my emphasis).

Palaver has come to feature prominently as a potential element of democratic governance in the writings of the Congolese historian and philosopher Ernest Wamba-dia-Wamba. Wiredu makes brief

---

democracy to the Western elective adversarial democracy" (Ramose 2004, 155).

8. Unlike the rest of Africa, in Ghana, Liberia, Nigeria, Sierra Leone, and West African pidgin, "palaver" can be used to refer to contentious arguments or unresolved trouble rather than compromise or consensus. This alternative meaning is sometimes attributed to linguistically challenged, expatriate, English-language speakers who misunderstood the indigenous meaning of the term. "In a great many contexts it [discussions by non-Africans where 'palaver' is rendered as 'trouble'] implies the [non-African] speaker's racist contempt or ethnocentric or class prejudice against the people spoken to or referred to" (Armstrong 1979, 14).

reference to him at several points (1996f, 151; 2004a, 21). Neverthe-less, the resemblance between the two appears significant and there-fore adds weight to both philosophers' claims that *consensus/palaver* is an original and widespread African practice.[9]

Other critics have suggested that even if consensual governance did distinguish Africa in times past, it was enacted at the level of the *individual* ethnic group. The typical African nation-state today is com-posed of a *multiplicity* of such groups. How are their sometimes ir-reconcilable, competing interests to be resolved so that these groups can contribute meaningfully to a consensual government of national unity? Even in the absence of political parties, why should it be pre-sumed that consensual governance would not face the same tribal-ism problem that has troubled African liberal democracies? It is not enough to say that with the appropriate adjustments to the machin-ery of consensual governance, consensus would carry over, and these groups would relate to one another as do members of a single ethnic group. The context is not the same.

Wiredu could respond that in his version of the nation-state, given the absence of political parties, this would be less of a problem. Rep-resentatives would be expected to sublimate their ethnic identities in the name of national consensus. But could this be better facilitated on both ideological and practical levels? To help Wiredu out here, perhaps it would be possible to tweak and transplant the idea of *overlapping consensus* that was introduced by John Rawls in an essay with that as its title (1987).

In the essay, Rawls is concerned with enabling justice—what he calls *political justice*—in a society where there is a plurality of real differences involving things like ethics, aesthetics, and religion. He suggests that this kind of diversity could be accommodated as long as there is *agreement on the part of its members to a foundational po-litical structure*: "We can live together in harmony despite conflicting

---

9. The similarities between consensus and palaver have been commented on at greater length by Richard H. Bell (2002, 112–17; 2007, chapter 6). Pieter Boele van Hensbroek (1999, 202–3) finds important differences as well as similarities between the two.

ideals of the good human being, of worthwhile living, of love and friendship, of ethical conduct, and the like, so long as we know that *we share a moral commitment to our society's basic structure*. . . . Rawls calls such a conception of justice—one that is not dependent on a more comprehensive worldview, but acceptable to adherents of diverse worldviews—a *political conception of justice*" (Pogge 2007, 34; my emphasis).

Wiredu might react positively to Rawls on this, or he might say this kind of explicit endorsement of political justice by the population represents a more nuanced articulation of the principle of sympathetic impartiality. Because the principle promotes human welfare and is ultimately environmentally derived, it is *natural* to human beings. If more explicitly acknowledged and publicly affirmed, it too could be used to introduce the idea of political justice that is Rawls's concern.

It seems that Wiredu might therefore say that the principle of sympathetic impartiality would be *more compatible* with consensual governance than liberal democracy as currently constituted. Political justice, now reframed as *political consensus*, would overlap cultural as well as ethnic differences. Rawls may have meant for this to apply to the conventional liberal democratic form of government, but why could it not also be incorporated into consensual democracy? Different ethnic groups—or rather, the citizens of which they are composed—commit to the *consensual nation-state* as a mutually beneficial platform to promote their interests despite differences arising from nonpolitical identities.

Is the principle of consensus accorded *genetic* status in Wiredu's philosophy? The genetic discoveries highlighted in previous chapters all have some form of universal status. They are seen as foundational to human society generally. Does consensus have that status? Empirically, at least, that does not seem to be the case. "That consensus is *universally desirable* among human beings is unlikely to be disputed. What is likely to evoke debate is whether it is a *necessary condition* for a viable political system" (Wiredu 1996o, 9; my emphasis). Even if true, desirable is not the same as being universally evidenced or complied with. Wiredu does not embrace some form of absolute environmental determinism. At various points, he indicates that humanity can also act against its own best interests. Perhaps the best way to make peace with this from a genetic point of view is to say that *the universal status of consensus may be pending.* Human evolution is not over and done with; it is an ongoing process. As time passes and our reflections are unconsciously or consciously refined about things that promote human welfare, consensual governance may yet emerge as something that is accorded universal status. Until then, as we witness its endorsement by some and disregard by others, that too can be characteristic of human evolution.

AFTERWORD

THOSE WHO KNEW OF KWASI Wiredu before reading this text almost certainly did so on the basis of his work in and on African philosophy. That Wiredu is concerned, among other things, to confront and disprove accounts of a "traditional" African intellect that could produce little of philosophical merit. He does not do this on the basis of rhetoric. He does it via subtle and exacting analyses of Africa's indigenous cultures to demonstrate that their languages, beliefs, and practices are reasonable and have philosophical merit. If one considers the manner in which Western academic philosophy has fed off of the raw material of that culture's languages and beliefs, such a strategy would seem to be perfectly in order. With this work, Wiredu is doing more than defending Africa's intellectual interests. He is also demonstrating to academic philosophy that its major issues of concern, the so-called problems of philosophy, can be illustrated in an insightful manner by content derived from Africa's indigenous cultures.

Wiredu's philosophical writings now encompass more than one hundred published essays, some of which are collected in his two edited volumes. These publications are listed in the bibliographies at the end of this volume, along with a variety of relevant secondary sources. Wiredu tells us that when familiar with these publications, African students of philosophy should be convinced that they do not have to be invested exclusively with Western languages and cultural content in order to encounter and master philosophy. Philosophy is there in their own languages and cultures.

Wiredu has sometimes been censured by colleagues for being too Western in his approach to African philosophy. If that sounds paradoxical, the point at issue is usually his reliance on analysis—on the clarification of ideas and the argumentation involved with their justification—in his writings.[1] But it is important to appreciate that his endorsement of analysis is conditional: "I believe that analysis is only one of the missions of philosophy" (2002b, 332). The significance of the qualification "only one" is that analysis must be supplemented by a genetic approach to the origins of the ideas being analyzed. For Wiredu, that is perhaps the most important and original dimension to his overall methodology. The elucidation of that genetic approach to philosophy has therefore been the subject of this little book.

This is a Wiredu who is fully engaged when he takes on someone like Quine with reference to his philosophy of logic, ontology, philosophy of language, and epistemology. It is a pity that the Nigerian journal *Second Order* was not on Quine's radar. Quine made a point of keeping up with his critics and often responded to them in print. The four "Logic and Ontology" essays therefore deserve much more attention than they have received. After all, most of the issues discussed in them and in this volume share in that timeless quality that is distinctive of the problems of philosophy.

An observation I will make at this point concerns his remarkable consistency. Wiredu's thoughts may be dispersed among numerous essays, but his adherence to specific foundational philosophical ideas and their consequences are there throughout. This gives the corpus coherence and unity that verge on the systemic. One therefore looks forward to the day when there will be a comprehensive edition of Wiredu's complete work as well as a secondary source that details the African material in the context of his analytic and genetic argumentation.

---

1. His essay "What Is Philosophy?" (1974) is the earliest example of his advocacy of analysis coupled with a genetic approach.

READING WIREDU BIBLIOGRAPHY

Abraham, W. E. 1962. *The Mind of Africa*. Chicago: University of Chicago Press.

Ajei, Martin O. 2012. "Problems with Wiredu's Empiricalism." *Legon Journal of the Humanities* 23:185–204.

———. 2016. "Kwasi Wiredu's Consensual Democracy: Prospects for Practice in Africa." *European Journal of Political Theory* 15, no. 4: 445–66.

Ani, E. I. 2010. "Cultural Universals and Particulars in the Philosophy of Kwasi Wiredu: Some Comments." *Thought and Practice* 2, no. 2: 19–47.

———. 2014. "On Agreed Actions without Agreed Notions." *South African Journal of Philosophy* 33, no. 3: 311–20.

———. 2018a. "The Question of Immanence in Kwasi Wiredu's Consensus Democracy." *Cultura* 15, no. 1: 161–76.

———. 2018b. "The Question of Rationality in Kwasi Wiredu's Consensual Democracy." In *Method, Substance, and the Future of African Philosophy*, 251–73. London: Palgrave Macmillan.

Appiah, Kwame Anthony. 1992. *In My Father's House: Africa in the Philosophy of Culture*. Oxford: Oxford University Press.

———. 2006. *Cosmopolitanism: Ethics in a World of Strangers*. New York: W. W. Norton.

Armstrong, Robert G. 1979. "The Public Meeting as a Means of Participation in Political and Social Activities." In *Socio-Political Aspects of the Palaver in Some African Countries*, 11–26. Paris: UNESCO.

Ayer, A. J. 1936. *Language, Truth and Logic*. London: Victor Gollanz.

Beattie, John. 1966. *Other Cultures: Aims, Methods and Achievements in Social Anthropology*. London: Routledge and Kegan Paul.

Bedu-Addo, J. T. 1981. "On the Concept of Truth in Akan." In *Philosophy in Africa: Trends and Perspectives*, edited by P. O. Bodunrin, 68–90. Ile-Ife, Nigeria: University of Ife Press.

Bell, Richard H. 2002. *Understanding African Philosophy*. New York: Routledge.

———. 2007. *Rethinking Justice: Restoring Our Humanity*. Lanham, MD: Lexington.

Bello, A. G. A. 1987. "Philosophy and an African Language." *Quest: An African Journal of Philosophy* 1, no. 1 (June): 5–11.

Blackburn, Simon. 2008. *Oxford Dictionary of Philosophy*, 2nd ed. Oxford: Oxford University Press.

Bricker, Philip. 2016. "Ontological Commitment." The Stanford Encyclopedia of Philosophy, edited by Edward N. Zalta. https://plato.stanford.edu/entries/ontological-commitment/.

Busia, K. A. 1967. *Africa in Search of Democracy*. London: Routledge and Kegan Paul.

———. 1995. "The Political Heritage of Africa in Search of Democracy." In *Readings in African Philosophy: An Akan Collection*, edited by Safro Kwame, 207–18. Lanham, MD: University Press of America.

Concise Oxford English Dictionary. 1964. Oxford: Clarendon.

Davidson, Donald, and J. Hintikka, eds. 2012. *Words and Objections: Essays on the Work of W. V. Quine*, vol. 21. Berlin: Springer Science & Business Media.

Dewey, John. 1902. "The Evolutionary Method Applied to Morality: 1. Its Scientific Necessity." *Philosophical Review* 11:107–24.

———. 2007. *Logic: The Theory of Inquiry*. New York: Saerchinger.

———. 2008. *The Later Works of John Dewey, Vol. 4, 1925–1953. 1929, The Quest for Certainty (Collected Works of John Dewey)*. Edited by Jo Ann Boydston. Carbondale: Southern Illinois University Press.

Durrell, Lawrence. 1991. *The Alexandria Quartet*. London: Penguin.

Eze, Emmanuel C. 1997. "Democracy or Consensus? A Response to Wiredu." In *Postcolonial African Philosophy*, edited by E. C. Eze, 313–23. Oxford: Blackwell.

Grayling, A. C., ed. 1998. *Philosophy 1*. Oxford: Oxford University Press.

Gyekye, Kwame. 1995. *An Essay on African Philosophical Thought: The Akan Conceptual Scheme*, rev. ed. Philadelphia: Temple University Press.

———. 2000. "Person and Community in African Thought." In *Philosophy from Africa*, edited by P. H. Coetzee and A. P. J. Roux, 317–36. Oxford: Oxford University Press.

———. 2013. *Philosophy, Culture and Vision.* Legon, Ghana: Sub-Saharan.

Hallen, Barry. 2006. *African Philosophy: The Analytic Approach.* Trenton, NJ: Africa World.

———. 2009. *A Short History of African Philosophy,* 2nd ed. Bloomington: Indiana University Press.

———. 2019. "Reconsidering the Case for Consensual Governance in Africa." *Second Order: An African Journal of Philosophy* 3, no. 1: 1–22.

Hallen, Barry, and J. Olubi Sodipo. 1997. *Knowledge, Belief, and Witchcraft: Analytic Experiments in African Philosophy,* rev. ed. Stanford, CA: Stanford University Press.

Herbst, Peter. 1963. "The Nature of Fact." In *Essays in Conceptual Analysis,* edited by Anthony Flew, 134–56. London: Macmillan.

Hollis, Martin, and Steven Lukes, eds. 1982. *Rationality and Relativism.* Oxford: Basil Blackwell.

Horton, Robin. 1993. *Patterns of Thought in Africa and the West: Essays on Magic, Religion and Science.* Cambridge: Cambridge University Press.

Hume, David. 2010. *Essays and Treatises on Several Subjects: Containing Philosophical Essays Concerning Human Understanding,* vol. II. Farmington Hills, MI: Gale ECCO.

Jacques, T. Carlos. 2012. "Alterity in the Discourse of African Philosophy: A Forgotten Absence." In *Reclaiming the Human Sciences and Humanities through African Perspectives,* edited by Helen Lauer and Kofi Anyidoho, 1017–30. Legon, Ghana: Sub-Saharan.

Karanja-Diejomaoh, Bi W. M. 1979. "The Palaver in Kenya." In *Socio-Political Aspects of the Palaver in Some African Countries,* 41–60. Paris: UNESCO.

Katz, J. J. 1988. "The Refutation of Indeterminacy." *The Journal of Philosophy* 85, no. 6 (May): 227–52.

Kaunda, Kenneth. 1966. *A Humanist in Africa.* London: Longman.

Kirk, Robert. 1986. *Translation Determined.* Oxford: Clarendon.

———. 2004. "Indeterminacy of Translation." In *The Cambridge Companion to Quine,* edited by Roger. F. Gibson, 151–80. Cambridge: Cambridge University Press.

Lauer, Helen. 2011. "Negotiating Precolonial History and Future Democracy: Kwasi Wiredu and His Critics." In *Identity Meets Nationality: Voices from the Humanities,* edited by Helen Lauer, Nana Aba Appiah Amfo, and Jemima Asabea Anderson, 174–89. Legon, Ghana: Sub-Saharan.

———. 2012a. "Wiredu and Eze on Good Governance." *Philosophia Africana* 14, no. 1 (September): 41–60.

———. 2012b. "Appendix: Jacques on Wiredu." In *Reclaiming the Human Sciences and Humanities through African Perspectives*, edited by Helen Lauer and Kofi Anyidoho, 1031–35. Legon, Ghana: Sub-Saharan.

Lijphart, Arend. 2012. *Patterns of Democracy*. New Haven, CT: Yale University.

Lukes, Steven. 2006. *Individualism*. University of Essex, UK: ECPR.

Masaka, Dennis. 2019. "Kwasi Wiredu's Consensual Democracy and One-Party Polities in Africa." *South African Journal of Philosophy* 38, no. 1: 68–78.

Masolo, D. A. 1994. *African Philosophy in Search of Identity*. Bloomington: Indiana University Press.

———. 2003. "Philosophy and Indigenous Knowledge: An African Perspective." Special issue, *Africa Today* 50, no. 2 (Fall/Winter): 21–38.

———. 2004. "Western and African Communitarianism: A Comparison." In *A Companion to African Philosophy*, edited by Kwasi Wiredu. London: Routledge, 483–98.

———. 2010. *Self and Community in a Changing World*. Bloomington: Indiana University Press.

———. 2014. "The Case for Communitarianism: A Reply to Critics." *Quest: An African Journal of Philosophy* 25, no. 1–2: 185–230.

Matolino, Bernard. 2013. "The Nature of Opposition in Kwasi Wiredu's Democracy by Consensus." *African Studies* 72, no. 1: 138–52.

———. 2016a. "Rationality and Consensus in Kwasi Wiredu's Traditional African Politics." *Theoria* 146:36–55.

———. 2016b. "Ending Party Cleavage for a Better Polity: Is Kwasi Wiredu's Non-Party Polity a Viable Alternative to a Party Policy?" *Acta Academica* 48, no. 2: 91–107.

———. 2018. *Consensus as Democracy in Africa*. Grahamstown, South Africa: NISC (Pty).

———. 2019. "Betwixt and Between: Kwasi Wiredu's Legacy in Postcolonial African Philosophy." *Journal of World Philosophies* 4 (Winter): 61–69.

Maurier, Henri. 1984. "Do We Have an African Philosophy?" In *African Philosophy: An Introduction*, 3rd ed., edited by Richard Wright, 25–40. Washington, DC: University Press of America.

Needham, Rodney. 1972. *Belief, Language, and Experience*. Oxford: Blackwell.

Ninsin, Kwame A. 2012. "Ghana Since the Mid-Twentieth Century: Tribe or Nation." In *Reclaiming the Human Sciences and Humanities through*

African Perspectives, edited by Helen Lauer and Kofi Anyidoho, 1116–41. Legon, Ghana: Sub-Saharan.

Nyerere, Julius K. 1968. *Ujamaa: Essays on Socialism*. New York: Oxford University Press.

Oxford Dictionary of Philosophy. 1994. Oxford: Oxford University Press.

Peil, Margaret. 1977. *Consensus and Conflict in African Societies*. London: Longman Group.

Pogge, Thomas W. 2007. *John Rawls: His Life and Theory of Justice*. Oxford: Oxford University Press.

Putnam, Hilary. 1975. "The Refutation of Conventionalism." In *Mind, Language and Reality*, 153–91. Cambridge: Cambridge University Press.

Quine, W. V. O. 1959. "Meaning and Translation." In *The Structure of Language*, edited by J. A. Fodor and J. J. Katz, 460–78. Englewood Cliffs, NJ: Prentice-Hall.

———. 1960. *Word and Object*. Cambridge, MA: MIT Press.

———. 1969a. "Epistemology Naturalized." In *Ontological Relativity and Other Essays*, 69–90. New York: Columbia University Press.

———. 1969b. "Existence and Quantification." In *Ontological Relativity and Other Essays*, 91–113. New York: Columbia University Press.

———. 1976a. "Logic as a Source of Syntactical Insights." In *The Ways of Paradox and Other Essays*, 44–49. Cambridge, MA: Harvard University Press.

———. 1976b. "A Logistical Approach to the Ontological Problem." In *The Ways of Paradox and Other Essays*, 197–202. Cambridge, MA: Harvard University Press.

———. 1980. "On What There Is." In *From a Logical Point of View*, 20–46. Cambridge, MA: Harvard University Press.

———. 1981. *Theories and Things*. Cambridge, MA: Belknap.

———. 1995. *From Stimulus to Science*. Cambridge, MA: Harvard University Press.

Ramose, Mogobe. 1992. "African Democratic Tradition: Oneness, Consensus and Openness: a Reply to Wamba-dia-Wamba." *Quest: An International African Journal of Philosophy* 6, no. 2: 63–83.

———. 2004. "In Search of an African Philosophy of Education." *South African Journal of Higher Education* 18, no. 3: 138–60.

Rawls, John. 1987. "The Idea of an Overlapping Consensus." *Oxford Journal of Legal Studies* 7, no. 1 (Spring): 1–25.

Reeve, John. 1974. "Wiredu and Objects: Some Objections." *Second Order* 3, no. 1: 29–37.

Scott, John, and Gordon Marshall, eds. 2005. *A Dictionary of Sociology.* Oxford: Oxford University Press.

Sharples, R. 1998. *Stoics, Epicureans and Sceptics.* London: Routledge.

Skinner, B. F. 1992. *Verbal Behavior.* Acton, MA: Copley.

Strawson, P. F. 1978. "Truth." In *An Introduction to Philosophical Inquiry,* 2nd ed., edited by Joseph Margolis, 293. New York: Alfred A. Knopff.

Taiwo, Olufemi. 1996. *Legal Naturalism.* Ithaca, NY: Cornell University Press.

UNESCO. 1979. *Socio-Political Aspects of the Palaver in Some African Countries.* Paris: UNESCO.

van Hensbroek, P. B. 1999. *Political Discourses in African Thought: 1860 to the Present.* Westport, CT: Praeger.

Wamba-dia-Wamba, E. 1983. "Philosophy in Africa: Challenges of the African Philosopher." *Mawazo* 5, no. 2 (December): 76–93.

———. 1985. "Experience of Democracy in Africa: Reflections on the Practice of Communalist Palaver as a Method of Resolving Contradictions among the People." *Philosophy and Social Action* 11, no. 3: 19–29.

———. 1992. "Beyond the Politics of Democracy in Africa." *Quest: Philosophical Discussions* 6, no. 1: 29–42.

———. 1994a. "Democracy in Africa and Democracy for Africa." *Codesria Bulletin* 2, no. 3.

———. 1994b. "Africa in Search of a New Mode of Politics." In *African Perspectives on Development: Controversies, Dilemmas, Openings,* edited by U. Himmelstrand et al., 249–61. London: James Curry.

Whorf, Benjamin Lee. 2011. *Language, Thought, and Reality.* Eastford, CT: Martino Fine Books.

Wiredu, Kwasi. 1973a. "Logic and Ontology, Part 1." *Second Order* 2, no. 1: 71–82. (Republished 2020 in *Second Order* 4, no. 1–2: 1–16.)

———. 1973b. "Logic and Ontology, Part 2." *Second Order* 2, no. 2: 21–38.

———. 1974. "Logic and Ontology, Part 3." *Second Order* 3, no. 2: 33–52.

———. 1975. "Logic and Ontology, Part 4." *Second Order* 4, no. 1: 25–43

———. 1977. "Philosophy and Our Culture." *Proceedings of the Ghana Academy of Arts and Sciences.* Accra, Ghana: Secretariat of the Academy of Arts and Sciences.

———. 1980a. "On an African Orientation in Philosophy." In *Philosophy and an African Culture,* 26–36. Cambridge: Cambridge University Press. (Previously published 1972 in *Second Order: An African Journal of Philosophy*: 3–13.)

————. 1980b. "How Not to Compare African Thought with Western Thought." In *Philosophy and an African Culture*, 37–50. Cambridge: Cambridge University Press. (Previously published 1976 in *Ch'indaba*; republished (a) 1984 in *African Philosophy: An Introduction* 3rd ed., edited by Richard Wright, 149–62. Lanham, MD: University Press of America; (b) 1995 in *African Philosophy: Selected Readings*, edited by Albert Mosley, 159–71. Englewood Cliffs, NJ: Prentice Hall; (c) 1997 in *Transition* 75/76, *The Anniversary Issue: Selections from Transition 1961–1975*: 320–27; and (d) 1997 in *Postcolonial African Philosophy*, edited by E. C. Eze, 193–99. Oxford: Blackwell Publishers.)

————. 1980c. "What Is Philosophy." In *Philosophy and an African Culture*, 139–73. Cambridge: Cambridge University Press. (Previously published 1974 in *Universitas*.)

————. 1980d. "Philosophy and an African Culture." In *Philosophy and an African Culture*, 1–25. Cambridge: Cambridge University Press.

————. 1980e. "Truth as Opinion." In *Philosophy and an African Culture*, 111–23. Cambridge: Cambridge University Press. (Previously published 1973 in *Universitas*.)

————. 1980f. "To Be Is to Be Known." In *Philosophy and an African Culture*, 124–38. Cambridge: Cambridge University Press. (Previously published 1974 in *Legon Journal of the Humanities* 1.)

————. 1980g. "In Defense of Opinion." In *Philosophy and an African Culture*, 174–88. Cambridge: Cambridge University Press.

————. 1985. "Replies to Critics." In *Philosophy in Africa: Trends and Perspectives*, edited by P. Bodunrin, 91–102. Ile-Ife, Nigeria: University of Ife Press.

————. 1987a. "The Concept of Mind with Particular Reference to the Language and Thought of the Akans of Ghana." In *Contemporary Philosophy, Africa (A New Survey)*, edited by Guttorm Floistad, 153–79. Dordrecht, South Africa: Springer. (Republished 1995 in *Readings in African Philosophy: An Akan Collection*, edited by Safro Kwame, 123–52. Lanham, MD: University Press of America.)

————. 1987b. "Truth: The Correspondence Theory of Judgment." *African Philosophical Inquiry* 1, no. 1: 19–30.

————. 1991. "On Defining African Philosophy." In *African Philosophy: The Essential Readings*, edited by Tsenay Serequeberhan, 87–110. New York: Paragon.

————. 1992. "The Moral Foundations of an African Culture." In *Person and Community: Ghanaian Philosophical Studies*, vol. 1, edited by Kwasi

Wiredu and Kwame Gyekye, 193–206. Washington, DC: Council for Research in Values and Philosophy. (Republished 1998 in *The African Philosophy Reader*, edited by P. H. Coetzee and A. P. J. Roux, 306–16. London: Routledge.)

———. 1995. "Knowledge, Truth and Fallibility." In *The Concept of Knowledge, Boston Studies in the Philosophy of Science*, vol. 170, edited by I. Kucuradi and R. S. Cohen, 127–48. Dordrecht, Neth.: Kluwer Academic Publishers.

———. 1996a. "A Philosophical Perspective on the Concept of Human Communication." In *Cultural Universals and Particulars: An African Perspective*, 13–20. Bloomington: Indiana University Press. (Previously published 1980 in *International Social Science Journal* 32, no. 2.)

———. 1996b. "Are There Cultural Universals?" In *Cultural Universals and Particulars: An African Perspective*, 21–33. Bloomington: Indiana University Press. (Previously published 1995 in *The Monist* 78, no. 1: 52–64; republished 1998 in *The African Philosophy Reader*, edited by P. H. Coetzee and A. P. J. Roux, 31–40. London: Routledge.)

———. 1996c. "Universalism and Particularism in Religion from an African Perspective." In *Cultural Universals and Particulars: An African Perspective*, 45–60. Bloomington: Indiana University Press. (Previously published 1990 in *Journal of Humanism and Ethical Religion* 3, no. 1.)

———. 1996d. "Formulating Modern Thought in African Languages: Some Theoretical Considerations." In *Cultural Universals and Particulars: An African Perspective*, 81–104. Bloomington: Indiana University Press. (Previously published 1992 in *The Surreptitious Speech*, edited by V. Y. Mudimbe, 301–32. Chicago: University of Chicago Press.)

———. 1996e. "African Philosophical Traditions: A Case Study of the Akan." In *Cultural Universals and Particulars: An African Perspective*, 113–35. Bloomington: Indiana University Press. (Previously published 1992–93 in *The Philosophical Forum* 34, no. 1–3.)

———. 1996f. "Post-Colonial African Philosophy." In *Cultural Universals and Particulars: An African Perspective*, 145–54. Bloomington: Indiana University Press. (Previously published 1995 in *Conceptual Decolonization in African Philosophy, Four Essays by Kwasi Wiredu*, edited by Olusegun Oladipo, 11–21. Ibadan, Nigeria: Hope.)

———. 1996g. "The Concept of Truth in the Akan Language." In *Cultural Universals and Particulars: An African Perspective*, 105–12. Bloomington:

Indiana University Press. (Previously published 1985 in *African Philosophy: Trends and Perspectives*, edited by P. Bodunrin, 43–54. Ile-Ife, Nigeria: University of Ife Press; republished (a) 1995 in *Readings in African Philosophy: An Akan Collection*, edited by Safro Kwame, 185–90. Lanham, MD: University Press of America; (b) 1997 in *Postcolonial African Philosophy*, edited by E. C. Eze, 176–80. Oxford: Blackwell Publishers; and (c) 1998 in *The African Philosophy Reader*, edited by P. H. Coetzee and A. P. J. Roux, 234–39. London: Routledge.)

———. 1996h. "Postscript: Reflections on Some Reactions." In *Cultural Universals and Particulars: An African Perspective*, 191–210. Bloomington: Indiana University Press.

———. 1996i. "Custom and Morality: A Comparative Analysis of Some African and Western Conceptions of Morals." In *Cultural Universals and Particulars: An African Perspective*, 61–78. Bloomington: Indiana University Press. (Previously published 1995 in *African Philosophy*, edited by Albert Mosley, 389–406. Englewood Cliffs, NJ: Prentice Hall.)

———. 1996j. "Democracy and Consensus: A Plea for a Non-Party Polity." In *Cultural Universals and Particulars: An African Perspective*, 182–90. Bloomington: Indiana University Press. (Previously published 1995 in *Centennial Review* 39, no. 1: 53–64; republished (a) 1997 in *Postcolonial African Philosophy*, edited by E. C. Eze, 303–12. Oxford: Blackwell Publishers; and (b) 1998 in *The African Philosophy Reader*, edited by P. H. Coetzee and A. P. J. Roux, 374–82. London: Routledge.)

———. 1996k. "The Need for Conceptual Decolonization in African Philosophy." In *Cultural Universals and Particulars: An African Perspective*, 136–44. Bloomington: Indiana University Press. (Previously published 1995 in *Conceptual Decolonization in African Philosophy, Four Essays by Kwasi Wiredu*, edited by Olusegun Oladipo, 22–32. Ibadan, Nigeria: Hope.)

———. 1996l. "An Akan Perspective on Human Rights." In *Cultural Universals and Particulars: An African Perspective*, 157–71. Bloomington: Indiana University Press. (Previously published 1990 in *Human Rights: Cross-Cultural Perspectives*, edited by Abdullahi Ahmed An-Na'im and Francis M. Deng. Washington, DC: The Brookings Institution.)

———. 1996m. "Philosophy and the Political Problem of Human Rights." In *Cultural Universals and Particulars: An African Perspective*, 172–81. Bloomington: Indiana University Press. (Previously published 1995 in

The Idea and Documents of Human Rights, edited by Ioanna Kucuradi. Ankara, Turkey: International Federation of Philosophical Societies and the Philosophical Society of Turkey.)

———. 1996n. "The Biological Foundation of Universal Norms." In *Cultural Universals and Particulars: An African Perspective*, 34–41. Bloomington: Indiana University Press.

———. 1996o. "Introduction: The Universal and the Particular." In *Cultural Universals and Particulars: An African Perspective*, 1–9. Bloomington: Indiana University Press.

———. 1998a. "The State, Civil Society and Democracy in Africa." *Quest: An International Journal of Philosophy* 22, no. 1 (June): 241–52.

———. 1998b. "The Moral Foundations of an African Culture." In *The African Philosophy Reader*, edited by P. H. Coetzee and A. J. P. Roux, 306–16. London: Routledge.

———. 1998c. "Toward Decolonizing African Philosophy and Religion." *African Studies Quarterly* 1, no. 4: 17–46.

———. 1999. "Society and Democracy in Africa." *New Political Science* 21, no. 1: 33–44.

———. 2001a. "Tradition, Democracy and Political Legitimacy in Contemporary Africa." In *Rewriting Africa: Toward Renaissance or Collapse?* edited by Eisei Kurimoto, 161–72. Japan Centre for Area Studies, JCAS Symposium Series n. 14. Osaka: National Museum of Ethnology.

———. 2001b. "Democracy by Consensus: Some Conceptual Considerations." *Philosophical Papers* 30, no. 3: 227–44.

———. 2002a. "Brief Remarks on Logical Positivism." In *The Third Way in African Philosophy: Essays in Honour of Kwasi Wiredu*, edited by Olusegun Oladipo, 315–22. Ibadan, Nigeria: Hope.

———. 2002b. "Kwasi Wiredu: The Making of a Philosopher." In *The Third Way in African Philosophy*, edited by Olusegun Oladipo, 323–40. Ibadan, Nigeria: Hope.

———. 2004a. "Introduction: African Philosophy in Our Time." In *A Companion to African Philosophy*, edited by Kwasi Wiredu, 1–27. London: Routledge.

———. 2004b. "Truth and an African Language." In *African Philosophy: New and Traditional Perspectives*, edited by Lee M. Brown, 35–50. Oxford: Oxford University Press.

———. 2004c. "L'empiricalisme: une philosophie africaine contemporaine." *Rue Descartes* 45, no. 3: 166–78.

———. 2005. "Reflections on Cultural Diversity." *Diogenes* 52, no. 1: 117–28.

———. 2007a. "Democracy by Consensus: Some Conceptual Considerations." *Socialism and Democracy* 21, no. 3: 155–70.

———. 2007b. "Truth and Dialogue." In *Cultures—Conflict—Analysis— Dialogue,* edited by. Christian Kanzian and Edmud Runggaldier, 123– 36. Publications of the Austrian Ludwig Wittgenstein Society, vol. 3 n.s. Heusenstamm, Ger.: Ontos.

———. 2008. "Social Philosophy in Postcolonial Africa: Some Preliminaries Concerning Communalism and Communitarianism." *South African Journal of Philosophy* 27, no. 4: 332–39.

———. 2011. "Empiricalism: The Empirical Character of an African Philosophy." In *Identity Meets Nationality: Voices from the Humanities,* edited by Helen Lauer, Nana Aba Appiah Amfo, and Jemima Asabea Anderson, 18–34. Accra, Ghana: Sub-Saharan.

———. 2012. "State, Civil Society and Democracy in Africa." In *Reclaiming the Human Sciences and Humanities through African Perspectives,* edited by Helen Lauer and Kofi Anyidoho, 1055–66. Legon, Ghana: Sub-Saharan.

Wiredu, Kwasi, and Kwame Gyekye, eds. 1992. *Person and Community: Ghanaian Philosophical Studies,* vol. 1. Washington, DC: Council for Research in Values and Philosophy.

Wittgenstein, Ludwig. 1958. *Philosophical Investigations,* translated by G. E. M. Anscombe. Oxford: Blackwell.

SUPPLEMENTARY WIREDU BIBLIOGRAPHY

Wiredu, Kwasi. 1970. "Kant's Synthetic Apriori in Geometry and the Rise of Non-Euclidean Geometries." *Kant-Studien* 61, no. 1–4: 5–27.

———. 1971. "Material Implication and 'If . . . Then.'" *International Logic Review* 3:252.

———. 1972. "A Note on Modal Quantification, Ontology and the Indenumerably Infinite." *Analysis* 32, no. 6 (June): 187.

———. 1972. "Material Implication and 'If-Then.'" *International Logic Review* 6 (December): 252.

———. 1973. "Deducibility and Inferability." *Mind* 82, no. 325: 31–55.

———. 1973. "On the Real Logical Structure of Lewis' 'Independent Proof.'" *Notre Dame Journal of Formal Logic* 14, no. 4 (October): 543–46.

———. 1974. "Carnap on Iterated Modalities." *Philosophy and Phenomenological Research* 35, no 2: 240–45.

———. 1974. "Classes and Sets." *Logique et Analyse* 17, no. 65 (January): 175.

———. 1974. "A Remark on a Certain Consequence of Connexive Logic for Zermelo's Set Theory." *Studia Logica* 33, no. 2: 127–30.

———. 1975. "Truth as a Logical Constant, with an Application to the Principle of Excluded Middle." *The Philosophical Quarterly* 25, no. 101: 305–17.

———. 1976. "Predication and Abstract Entities." *Legon Journal of the Humanities* 2.

———. 1976. "On the Formal Character of Logic." *Ghana Social Science Journal* 3–4 (May).

———. 1976. "On Reductio ad Absurdum Proofs." *International Logic Review* 13 (June): 90.

———. 1976. "Paradoxes." *Second Order* 5, no. 2: 3–26.

———. 1979. "On the Necessity of S4." *Notre Dame Journal of Formal Logic* 20:689–94.

———. 1980. "What Can Philosophy Do for Africa?" In *Philosophy and an African Culture*, 51–62. Cambridge: Cambridge University Press.

———. 1980. "Marxism, Philosophy and Ideology." In *Philosophy and an African Culture*, 63–87. Cambridge: Cambridge University Press.

———. 1980. "In Praise of Utopianism." In *Philosophy and an African Culture*, 88–98. Cambridge: Cambridge University Press.

———. 1980. "Philosophy, Mysticism and Rationality." In *Philosophy and an African Culture*, 99–110. Cambridge: Cambridge University Press.

———. 1980. "Truth: A Dialogue." In *Philosophy and an African Culture*, 189–232. Cambridge: Cambridge University Press.

———. 1981. "Philosophy in Africa Today." In *Into the 80s: The Proceedings of the Eleventh Annual Conference of the Canadian Association of African Studies*, edited by D. Ray, P. Shinnie, and D. Williams, 176–84. Calgary: University of Calgary, Tantalus Research.

———. 1983. "Morality and Religion in Akan Thought." In *Philosophy and Cultures*, edited by H. Odera Oruka and D. A. Masolo, 6–13. Nairobi: Bookwise.

———. 1984. "Philosophical Research and Teaching in Africa: Some Suggestions." In *Teaching and Research in Philosophy: Africa*. Paris: UNESCO.

———. 1984. "Survey: Philosophy Teaching and Research in English-Speaking Africa." In *Teaching and Research in Philosophy: Africa*. Paris: UNESCO.

———. 1984. "Some Issues in Philosophy in Africa Today." In *Teaching and Research in Philosophy: Africa*. Paris: UNESCO.

———. 1985. "Problems in Africa's Self-Identification in the Contemporary World." In *Africa and the Problem of Its Identity*, edited by A. Diemer and P. Hountondji, 213–22. New York: Peter Lang.

———. 1986. "The Question of Violence in Contemporary African Thought." *Praxis International* 6, no. 3: 373–81.

———. 1989. "Death and the Afterlife in African Culture." In *Death and Dying: Cross-Cultural and Multi-Disciplinary Views*, edited by A. Berger et al., 24–37. Philadelphia: Charles.

———. 1990. "On the Question of the Right to Die: An African View." In *To Die or Not to Die?: Cross-Disciplinary, Cultural, and Legal Perspectives on the Right to Choose Death*, edited by Arthur S. Berger and Joyce Berger, 43–58. New York: Praeger.

———. 1990. "Universalism and Particularism in Religion from an African Perspective." *Journal of Humanism and Ethical Religion* 3, no. 1. Reprinted in *Self, Cosmos, God*, edited by D. Kolak and R. Martin. New York: Harcourt Brace Jovanovich College, 1992.

———. 1991. "Morality and Religion in Akan Thought." In *African American Humanism: An Anthology*, edited by Norm Allen Jr., 210–22. New York: Prometheus.

———. 1992. "The African Concept of Personhood." In *African American Perspectives on Biomedical Ethics*, edited by Harley E. Flack and Edmund D. Pellegrino, 104–17. Washington, DC: Georgetown University Press.

———. 1992. "Introduction: The Ghanaian Tradition of Philosophy." In *Person and Community: Ghanaian Philosophical Studies*, vol. 1, edited by Kwasi Wiredu and Kwame Gyekye, 1–12. Washington, DC: Council for Research in Values and Philosophy.

———. 1992. "Problems in Africa's Self-Definition in the Contemporary World." In *Person and Community: Ghanaian Philosophical Studies*, vol. 1, edited by Kwasi Wiredu and Kwame Gyekye, 59–72. Washington, DC: Council for Research in Values and Philosophy.

———. 1992. "Death and the Afterlife in African Culture." In *Person and Community: Ghanaian Philosophical Studies*, vol. 1, edited by Kwasi Wiredu and Kwame Gyekye, 137–52. Washington, DC: Council for Research in Values and Philosophy.

———. 1992. "Science, Technology and Humane Values." In *Paths to Human Flourishing: Philosophical Perspectives*, 35–62. Seoul: Korean Philosophical Association.

———. 1993. "Canons of Conceptualization. *The Monist* 76, no. 4: 450–76.

———. 1995. "On the Idea of a Global Ethic." *Journal of Global Ethics* 1, no. 1: 45–51.

———. 1995. *Conceptual Decolonization in African Philosophy: Four Essays by Kwasi Wiredu*. Introduced and edited by Olusegun Oladipo. Ibadan, Nigeria: Hope.

———. 1995. "Metaphysics in Africa." In *A Companion to Metaphysics*, edited by J. Kim and E. Sosa, 415–18. Oxford: Blackwell.

———. 1995. "Particularistic Studies of African Philosophies as an Aid to Decolonization." In *Decolonizing the Mind: Proceedings of the Colloquium Held at Unisa, October 1995*, edited by J. Malherbe. Pretoria: Research Unit for African Philosophy. Republished in *The African Philosophy Reader*, edited by P. H. Coetzee and A. P. J. Roux, 186–204. London: Routledge, 1998.

———. 1995. "On Decolonizing African Religions." In *Decolonizing the Mind: Proceedings of the Colloquium Held at Unisa, October 1995*, edited by J. Malherbe. Pretoria: Research Unit for African Philosophy. Republished in *The African Philosophy Reader*, edited by P. H. Coetzee and A. P. J. Roux, 186–204. London: Routledge, 1998.

———. 1995. "Philosophy, Humankind and the Environment." In *Philosophy of Nature and Environmental Ethics*. Volume 1 of *Philosophy, Humanity and Ecology*, edited by H. Odera Oruka, 30–48. Nairobi: African Center for Technology Studies.

———. 1995. "Particularistic Studies of African Philosophies as an Aid to Decolonization." In *Decolonizing the Mind: Proceedings of the Colloquium Held at Unisa, October 1995*, edited by J. Malherbe. Pretoria: Research Unit for African Philosophy. Republished in *The African Philosophy Reader*, edited by P. H. Coetzee and A. P. J. Roux, 186–204. London: Routledge, 1998.

———. 1995. "Custom and Morality: A Comparative Analysis of Some African and Western Conceptions of Morals." In *African Philosophy: Selected Readings*, edited by Albert Mosley, 389–406. Englewood Cliffs, NJ: Prentice Hall.

———. 1996. "Time and African Thought." In *Time and Temporality in Intercultural Perspective*, edited by D. Tiemersma and H. A. F. Osterling, 127–36. Atlanta: Rodopi.

———. 1996. "Reply to English and Hamme." *Journal of Social Philosophy* 27, no. 2: 234–43.

———. 1997. "African Philosophy and Inter-Cultural Dialogue." *Quest: An International African Journal of Philosophy* 11, no. 1–2: 29–42.

———. 1998. "African Philosophy: Anglophone." In *Encyclopedia of Philosophy*, edited by Edward Craig, 98. London: Routledge.

———. 1998. "Akan Philosophical Psychology." In *Encyclopedia of Philosophy*, edited by Edward Craig, 138. London: Routledge.

———. 1998. "Can Philosophy Be Intercultural? An African Viewpoint." *Diogenes* 46, no. 4: 147–67.

———. 2000. "Our Problem of Knowledge: Brief Reflections on Knowledge and Development in Africa." In *African Philosophy as Cultural Inquiry*, edited by Ivan Karp and D. A. Masolo, 181–86. Bloomington: Indiana University Press.

———. 2002. "Conceptual Decolonization as an Imperative in Contemporary African Philosophy: Some Personal Reflections." *Rue Descartes* 36, no. 2: 53–64.

———. 2003. "Some Comments on Contemporary African Philosophy." *Florida Philosophical Review* 3, no. 1: 91–96.

———. 2004. "Amo's Critique of Descartes' Philosophy of Mind." In *A Companion to African Philosophy*, 200–206. Oxford: Blackwell Publishing.

———. 2004. "Prolegomena to an African Philosophy of Education: Perspectives on Higher Education." *South African Journal of Higher Education* 18, no. 3 (January): 17–26.

———. 2005. "Empiricalism: Contemporary Philosophical Thought." *Filozofski Vestnik* 26, no. 3: 187–200.

———. 2007. "The Role of Philosophy in Intercultural Dialogue: An African Perspective." In *The Proceedings of the Twenty-First World Congress of Philosophy* vol. 13 (January), 47–53.

———. 2007. "Philosophy and Authenticity." *Shibboleths: A Journal of Comparative Theory* 1, no. 2: 72–80.

———. 2009. "An Oral Philosophy of Personhood: Comments on Philosophy and Orality." *Research in African Literatures* 40, no. 1 (Spring): 8–18.

———. 2010. "African Religions from a Philosophical Point of View." In *A Companion to Philosophy of Religion*, 2nd ed., edited by Charles Taliaferro, Paul Draper, and Philip L. Quinn, 34–43. Oxford: Wiley-Blackwell.

———. 2010. "African Religions." In *Companion to Philosophy of Religion*, edited by Chad Meister and Paul Copan, 29–39. London: Routledge.

———. 2010. "An African Religious Perspective." In *The Oxford Handbook of Religious Diversity*, edited by Chad V. Meister, 337–50. Oxford: Oxford University Press.

———. 2011. "The Humanities and the Idea of National Identity." In *Philosophical Foundations of the African Humanities through Postcolonial Perspectives*, edited by Helen Yitah and Helen Lauer, 1–17. Leiden, Neth.: Brill Rodopi.

———. 2013. "The Concept of a Person as both Descriptive
and Normative." In *African-American Perspectives and
Philosophical Traditions*, edited by John Pittman, 48–62. London:
Routledge.

Wiredu, Kwasi, ed. 2004. *A Companion to African Philosophy*. Oxford:
Blackwell.

COMMENTARIES AND
RELEVANT TEXTS

Ani, E. I. 2014. "On Traditional African Consensual Rationality." *Journal of Political Philosophy* 22, no. 3: 342–65.

———. 2017/2018. "Theistic Humanism and a Critique of Wiredu's Notion of Supernaturalism." *Critical Research on Religion* 6, no. 1: 69–84.

———. 2018. "Africa and Deliberative Politics." In *The Oxford Handbook of Deliberative Democracy*, edited by Andre Bachtiger, John Dryzek, Jane Mansbridge, and Mark Warren, 819–28. Oxford: Oxford University Press.

Ani, E. I., and Edwin Etieyibo, eds. 2020. *Deciding in Unison: Themes in Consensual Democracy in Africa*. Wilmington, DE: Vernon.

Ansah, Richard, and Modestha Mensah. 2019. "Gyekye's Moderate Communitarianism." OGIRISI 15:1–26. http://dx.doi.org/10.4314/og .v15i1.1.

Avineri, S., and A. de-Shalit, eds. 1992. *Communitarianism and Individualism*. Oxford: Oxford University Press.

Barber, Karin. 2007. *The Anthropology of Texts, Persons and Publics: Oral and Written Culture in Africa and Beyond*. Cambridge: Cambridge University Press.

Bell, D. A. 1993. *Communitarianism and Its Critics*. Oxford: Oxford University Press.

———. 1995. "A Communitarian Critique of Authoritarianism." *Society* 32, no. 5: 38–43.

———. 1997. "A Communitarian Critique of Authoritarianism: The Case of Singapore." *Political Theory* 25, no. 1 (February): 6–32.

Bell, Richard H. 1984. "Wittgenstein's Anthropology: Self-Understanding and Understanding Other Cultures." *Philosophical Investigations* 7, no. 4 (October): 295–312.

Bello, A. G. A. 1993. "Rationality, Myth and Philosophy in Africa." *Ibadan Journal of Humanistic Studies* 6 (August): 88–93.

———. 2002. "On the Concepts of Rationality and Communalism in African Scholarship." In *The Third Way in African Philosophy: Essays in Honour of Kwasi Wiredu*, edited by Olusegun Oladipo, 235–51. Ibadan, Nigeria: Hope.

———. 2004. "Some Methodological Controversies in African Philosophy." In *A Companion to African Philosophy*, edited by Kwasi Wiredu, 200–206. London: Routledge.

Carman, Mary. 2016. "A Defense of Wiredu's Project of Conceptual Decolonisation." *South African Journal of Philosophy* 35, no. 2: 235–48.

Cavell, Stanley. 1979. *The Claim of Reason*. Oxford: Oxford University Press.

Chemhuru, M. 2013. "Consensus and Conflict Resolution in Post-colonial Zimbabwe: Philosophical Reflections on an Indigenous Method of Conflict Resolution." *Journal on African Philosophy* 7:32–41.

Ciaffa, J. A. 2008. "Tradition and Modernity in Postcolonial African Philosophy." *Humanitas* 21, no. 1–2: 121–45.

Cioffi, Frank. 1998. *Wittgenstein on Freud and Frazer*. Cambridge: Cambridge University Press.

Coetzee, Pieter. 2003. "Particularity in Morality and Its Relation to Community." In *Philosophy from Africa: a Text with Readings*, edited by P. H. Coetzee and A. P. J. Roux, 273–86. Cape Town: Oxford University Press.

Cohen, J. 1989. "Deliberative Democracy and Democratic Legitimacy." In *The Good Polity*, edited by A. Hamlin and P. Petit, 17–34. Oxford: Blackwell.

Cooke, Maeve. 2000. "Five Arguments for Deliberative Democarcy." *Political Studies* 48:947–69.

Deng, F. M. 2005. "Human Rights in the African Context." In *A Companion to African Philosophy*, edited by Kwasi Wiredu, 499–508. London: Routledge.

Diagne, S. B. 2009. "Individual, Community, and Human Rights." *Transition: An International Review* 101:8–15.

Eboh, M. P. 1993. "Democracy with an African Flair: A Reply to Wamba-dia-Wamba." *Quest: An International African Journal of Philosophy* 7, no. 1: 92–99.

Edet, Mesembe I. 2015. "The Question of Conceptual Decolonization
    in African Philosophy and the Problem of the Language of African
    Philosophy." In *Atuolu Omalu: Some Unanswered Questions in
    Contemporary African Philosophy*, edited by Jonathan O. Chimakonam,
    197–218. Lanham, MD: University Press of America.

English, Parker, and Nancy Steele Hamme. 1996. "Using Art History
    and Philosophy to Compare a Traditional and Contemporary Form of
    African Moral Thought." *Journal of Social Philosophy* 27, no. 2: 204–33.

Etieyibo, E., and P. Ikuenobe, eds. 2020. *Menkiti on Community and
    Becoming a Person*. Lanham, MD: Lexington.

Etzioni, A. 2003. "Communitarianism." In *Encyclopedia of Community:
    From the Village to the Virtual World*, vol. 1, edited by K. Christensen
    and D. Levinson, 224–28. Los Angeles: Sage.

Eze, Michael. 2008. "What Is African Communitarianism? Against
    Consensus as a Regulative Ideal." *South African Journal of Philosophy*
    27, no. 4: 106–19.

Fabian, Johannes. 1983. *Time and the Other: How Anthropology Makes Its
    Object*. New York: Columbia University Press.

———. 1990. "Presence and Representation: The Other and
    Anthropological Writing." *Critical Inquiry* 16, no. 4: 753–72.

———. 1995. "Ethnographic Misunderstanding and the Perils of
    Context." *American Anthropologist* 97, no. 1: 41–50.

Famakinwa, J. O. 2010. "How Moderate Is Kwame Gyekye's Moderate
    Communitarianism." *Thought and Practice* 22, no. 2: 65–77.

———. 2010. "The Moderate Communitarian Individual and the
    Primacy of Duties." *Theoria* 76:152–66.

Fasiku, G. 2008. "African Philosophy and the Method of Ordinary
    Language Philosophy." *African Journal of Political Science and
    International Relations* 2, no. 4 (December): 85–90.

Fatton, R., Jr. 1990. "Liberal Democracy in Africa." *Political Science
    Quarterly* 105, no. 3: 455–73.

Fayemi, A. K. 2010. "A Critique of Consensual Democracy and Human
    Rights in Kwasi Wiredu's Philosophy." *Lumina: An Interdisciplinary
    Research and Scholarly Journal* 21, no. 1: 1–13.

———. 2010. "Cultural Universals and Particulars in the Philosophy of
    Kwasi Wiredu: Some Comments." *Thought and Practice* 2, no. 2: 19–47.

———. 2011. "A Critique of Cultural Universals and Particulars in Kwasi
    Wiredu's Philosophy." *Trames: A Journal of the Humanities and Social
    Sciences* 15, no. 3: 259–76.

———. 2020. "Against Consensual Governance in Africa: A Reply to Barry Hallen." *Second Order* 4, no. 1–2: 33–51.

Flikschuh, K. 2014. "The Idea of Philosophical Fieldwork: Global Justice, Moral Ignorance, and Intellectual Attitudes." *Journal of Political Philosophy* 22, no. 1: 1–26.

Gaudet, E. 2006. *Quine on Meaning: The Indeterminacy of Translation.* London: A & C Black.

Gbadegesin, E. O., Y. K. Salami, and K. Abimbola, eds. 2016. *Exploring the Ethics of Individualism and Communitarianism.* Mitchellville, MD: Harvest Day.

Gbadegesin, S. 1991. "Individuality, Community, and the Moral Order." In *African Philosophy.* New York: Peter Lang, 61–82. Reprinted in *The African Philosophy Reader*, edited by P. H. Coetzee and A. P. J. Roux, 292–305. London: Routledge, 1998.

Geertz, Clifford. 1973. *The Interpretation of Cultures.* New York: Basic.

———. 1977. "Found in Translation: On the Social History of the Moral Imagination." *The Georgia Review* 31 (Winter): 788–810.

Graness, Anke. 2002. "Wiredu's Ethics of Consensus: Model for a Global Ethics." In *The Third Way in African Philosophy: Essays in Honour of Kwasi Wiredu*, edited by Olusegun Oladipo, 252–68. Ibadan, Nigeria: Hope.

Gyekye, Kwame. 1977. "Akan Language and the Materialism Thesis: A Short Essay on the Relations between Philosophy and Language." *Studies in Language* 1, no. 1: 237–44.

———. 1978. "Akan Concept of a Person." *International Philosophical Quarterly* 18, no. 3 (September): 277–87.

———. 1991. "Man as a Moral Subject: The Perspective of an African Philosophical Anthropology." In *The Quest for Man: The Topicality of Philosophical Anthropology*, edited by Joris Van Nispen and Douwe Tiemersma, 135–39. Assen, Neth.: Van Gorcum.

———. 1997. *Tradition and Modernity: Philosophical Reflections on the African Experience.* New York: Oxford University Press.

Habermas, Jurgen. 1990. *The Philosophical Discourse of Modernity*, translated by Frederick G. Lawrence. Cambridge, MA: MIT Press.

Horton, Robin, and Ruth Finnegan, eds. 1973. *Modes of Thought: Essays on Thinking in Western and Non-Western Societies.* London: Faber and Faber.

Hountondji, P. J., 1983. *African Philosophy: Myth and Reality.* Bloomington: Indiana University Press.

———. 2002. *The Struggle for Meaning: Reflections on Philosophy, Culture, and Democracy in Africa*. Athens: Ohio University Press.

———. 2009. "Knowledge of Africa, Knowledge by Africans: Two Perspectives on African Studies." *RCCS Annual Review* 1:1–11.

Ikuenobe, Polycarp. 1998. "A Defense of Epistemic Authoritarianism in Traditional African Cultures." *Journal of Philosophical Research* 23:417–40.

———. 2002. "Moral Epistemology, Relativism, African Cultures, and the Distinction between Custom and Morality." *Journal of Philosophical Research* 27:641–69.

———. 2004. "Logical Positivism, Analytic Method, and Criticisms of Ethnophilosophy." *Metaphilosophy* 35, no. 4: 479–503.

———. 2006. *Philosophical Perspectives on Communalism and Morality in African Traditions*. Lanham, MD: Lexington.

Irele, Abiola. 1986. "Contemporary Thought in French Speaking Africa." In *Africa and the West: The Legacies of Empire*, edited by Isaac James Mowoe and Richard Bjornson, translated by R. Bjornson, 121–58. New York: Greenwood.

Jeffers, Chike. 2011. "Kwasi Wiredu et la Question du Nationalisme Culturel." *Critique* 8:639–49.

Keita, Lesenta. 1997. "A Review of Kwasi Wiredu's *Cultural Universals and Particulars*." *Quest: An International African Journal of Philosophy* 11, no. 182: 171–85.

Kwame, Safro, ed. 1995. *Readings in African Philosophy: An Akan Collection*. Lanham, MD: University Press of America.

Kresse, K. 1999. "The Problem of How to Use African Language for African Thought: On a Multilingual Perspective in African Philosophy." *African Philosophy* 12, no. 1: 27–36.

Lauer, Helen. 2007. "Depreciating African Political Culture." *Journal of Black Studies* 38, no. 2: 288–307.

Lukes, Steven. 2000. "Different Cultures, Different Rationalities." *History of the Human Sciences* 13, no. 1 (February): 5–18.

———. 2007. "Apparently Irrational Beliefs." In *Handbook of Philosophy, Anthropology and Sociology*, edited by Stephen Turner and Mark Risjord, 591–606. Amsterdam: Elsevier.

Mamdani, Mahmood. 1996. *Citizen and Subject: Contemporary Africa and the Legacy of Late Colonialism*. Princeton, NJ: Princeton University Press.

Martens, David B. 2019. "Wiredu Contra Lewis on the Right Modal Logic." *Organon F* 26, no. 3: 474–490.

Martinon, J. P. 2019. "Race and Universality: Meillassoux Meets Eze and Wiredu." *Pli: The Warwick Journal of Philosophy*, 30:49–71.

Masolo, D. A. 1992. "History and the Modernization of African Philosophy: A Reading of Kwasi Wiredu." In *Postkoloniales Philosophieren: Afrika*, edited by H. Nagl Docekal and F. M. Wimmer, 65–100. Wien: Oldenbourg.

———. 1999. "Rethinking Communities in a Global Context." *African Philosophy* 12, no. 1: 51–68.

———. 2001. "Communitarianism: an African Perspective." In *The Proceedings of the World Philosophy Congress*, vol. 12, 209–28.

———. 2002. "Community, Identity, and the Cultural Space." *Rue Descartes* 36, no. 3: 21–51.

———. 2002. "From Village to Global Contexts: Ideas, Types, and the Making of Communities." In *Diversity and Community: An Interdisciplinary Reader*, edited by Philip Alperson, 88–115. New York: Blackwell.

———. 2002. "Rethinking Communities in a Global Context." In *Philosophy from Africa: A Text with Readings*, 2nd. ed., edited by P. H. Coetzee and A. P. J. Roux, 558–73. Cape Town: Oxford University Press.

———. 2009. "Narrative and Experience of Community as Philosophy of Culture." *Thought and Practice* 1, no. 1: 43–68.

———. 2017. "Africanizing Philosophy: Wiredu, Hountondji, and Mudimbe." In *The Palgrave Handbook of African Philosophy*, edited by Adeshina Afolayan and Toyin Falola, 61–74. New York: Palgrave Macmillan.

Matolino, B. 2009. "Radicals versus Moderates: A Critique of Gyekye's Moderate Communitarianism." *South African Journal of Philosophy* 28, no. 2: 160–70.

———. 2009. "A Response to Eze's Critique of Wiredu's Consensual Democracy." *South African Journal of Philosophy* 28, no. 1: 34–42.

———. 2013. "The Nature of Opposition in Kwasi Wiredu's Democracy by Consensus." *African Studies* 72, no. 1: 138–52.

———. 2019. *Afro-Communitarian Democracy*. Lanham, MD: Lexington.

Menkiti, I. A. 1984. "Person and Community in African Traditional Thought. *African Philosophy: An Introduction*, 3rd ed., edited by Richard Wright, 171–82. Lanham, MD: University Press of America.

———. 2005. "On the Normative Conception of a Person." In *A Companion to African Philosophy*, edited by Kwasi Wiredu, 324–31. Oxford: Blackwell.

Molefe, Motsamai. 2016. "A Critique of Kwasi Wiredu's Humanism and Impartiality." *Acta Academica* 48:89–108.

———. 2016. "African Ethics and Partiality." *Phronimon* 17:104–22.

———. 2017. "An African Perspective on the Partiality and Impartiality Debate: Insights from Kwasi Wiredu's Moral Philosophy." *South African Journal of Philosophy* 36, no. 4: 470–82.

———. 2017. "Community, Communism, Communitarianism: An African Intervention." In *The Palgrave Handbook of African Philosophy*, edited by Adeshina Afolayan and Toyin Falola, 461–73. New York: Palgrave Macmillan.

Mudimbe, V. Y. 1988. *The Invention of Africa: Gnosis, Philosophy and the Order of Knowledge*. Bloomington: Indiana University Press.

———, ed. 1989. *The Surreptitious Speech: Presence Africaine and the Politics of Otherness*. Chicago: University of Chicago Press.

———. 1994. *The Idea of Africa*. Bloomington: Indiana University Press.

Mukandala, R. 2001. "The State of African Democracy: Status, Prospects, Challenges." *African Journal of Political Science* 6, no. 2: 1–10.

Mulhall, Stephen. 1990. *On Being in the World: Wittgenstein and Heidegger on Seeing Aspects*. London: Routledge.

Neequaye, George Kotei. 2020. "Ethical Thought of Kwasi Wiredu and Kwame Gyekye." In *The Palgrave Handbook of African Social Ethics*, edited by Adeshina Afolayan and Toyin Falola, 423–435. London: Palgrave Macmillan.

Oguejiofor, J. Obi. 2002. "Kwasi Wiredu and the Possibility of a History of African Philosophy." In *The Third Way in African Philosophy: Essays in Honour of Kwasi Wiredu*, edited by Olusegun Oladipo, 117–34. Ibadan, Nigeria: Hope.

Oke, Moses. 1988. "Wiredu's Theory and Practice of African Philosophy." *Second Order* 1, no. 1: 91–107.

———. 2002. "Modeling the Contemporary African Philosopher: Kwasi Wiredu in Focus." In *The Third Way in African Philosophy: Essays in Honour of Kwasi Wiredu*, edited by Olusegun Oladipo, 19–35. Ibadan, Nigeria: Hope.

Oladipo, Olusegun. 1995. "Introduction." In *Conceptual Decolonization in African Philosophy*. Ibadan, Nigeria: Hope.

———. 1996. *Philosophy and the African Experience: The Contributions of Kwasi Wiredu.* Ibadan, Nigeria: Hope.

———. 2002. "Introduction: The Third Way in African Philosophy." In *The Third Way in African Philosophy: Essays in Honour of Kwasi Wiredu,* edited by Olusegun Oladipo, 11–16. Ibadan, Nigeria: Hope.

———. 2002. "Kwasi Wiredu's Idea of African Philosophy." In *The Third Way in African Philosophy: Essays in Honour of Kwasi Wiredu,* edited by Olusegun Oladipo, 36–60. Ibadan, Nigeria: Hope.

Olanipekun, Victor Olusola. 2020. "Democracy and Consensus in Traditional Africa: A Critique of Kwasi Wiredu." *Inkanyiso: Journal of Humanities and Social Sciences* 12, no. 1: 1–10.

Onah, Godfrey I. 2002. "The Universal and the Particular in Wiredu's Philosophy of Human Nature." In *The Third Way in African Philosophy: Essays in Honour of Kwasi Wiredu,* edited by Olusegun Oladipo, 61–97. Ibadan, Nigeria: Hope.

Oruka, H. Odera. 1988. "For the Sake of Truth: A Response to Wiredu's Critique of 'Truth and Belief,'" *Quest: Philosophical Discussions* 2, no. 2: 3–22.

———, ed. 1990. *Sage Philosophy: Indigenous Thinkers and Modern Debate on African Philosophy.* Leiden, Neth.: E. J. Brill.

———. 1990. *Trends in Contemporary African Philosophy.* Nairobi: Shirikon.

———. 1995. "Cultural Fundamentals in Philosophy: Obstacles in Philosophical Dialogue." In *The Concept of Knowledge: Boston Studies in the Philosophy of Science,* edited by I. Kucuradi and R. S. Cohen, 167–81. Dordrecht, Neth.: Kluwer Academic.

———. 2002. "Four Trends in Current African Philosophy." In *Philosophy from Africa: A Text with Readings,* 2nd ed., edited by P. H. Coetzee and A. J. P. Roux, 120–24. Oxford: Oxford University Press.

Osha, S. 2005. "Kwasi Wiredu: Philosophy in the African Way." *African Renaissance* 2, no. 5: 106–10.

———. 2005. *Kwasi Wiredu and Beyond: The Text, Writing and Thought in Africa.* Dakar: CODESRIA.

Owomoyela, O. 1987. "Africa and the Imperative of Philosophy: A Skeptical Consideration." *African Studies Review* 30, no. 1: 79–100.

Oyowe, O. 2018. "Personhood and the Strongly Normative Constraint." *Philosophy East and West* 68, no. 3: 783–801.

Oyowe, O., and Olga Yurkivska. 2014. "Can a Communitarian Concept of African Personhood Be Both Relational and Gender-Neutral?" *South African Journal of Philosophy* 33, no. 1: 85–99.

Pagin, Peter. 2014. "Indeterminacy of Translation." In *Blackwell Companions to Philosophy: A Companion to W. V. O. Quine*, edited by Gilbert Harman and Ernest Lepore, 236–62. Oxford: Wiley Blackwell.

Quayson, Ato. 2000. *Postcolonialism: Theory, Practice and Process*. Oxford: Blackwell.

Ramose, M. B. 2009. "Towards Emancipative Politics in Modern Africa." In *African Ethics: An Anthology of Comparative and Applied Ethics*, 412–26. Scottsville, South Africa: University of KwaZulu-Natal Press.

Rattray, R. S. 1969. *Ashanti Law and Constitution*. Oxford: Clarendon.

Reeve, John. 1974. "Wiredu and Objects: Some Objections." *Second Order* 3, no. 1: 29–37.

Rettova, A. 2002. "The Role of African Languages in African Philosophy." *Rue Descartes* 2:129–50.

Rodrik, D. 2016. "Is Liberal Democracy Feasible in Developing Countries?" *Studies in Comparative International Development* 51:50–59.

Serequeberhan, Tsenay. 1994. *The Hermeneutics of African Philosophy*. London: Routledge.

Sklar, R. L. 1983. "Democracy in Africa." *African Studies Review* 26, no. 3–4: 11–24.

Sogolo, G. 1988. "African Philosophers and African Philosophy." *Second Order* 1, no. 1: 109–13.

———. 1990. "Options in African Philosophy." *Philosophy* 65, no. 251: 39–52.

———. 1993. *Foundations of African Philosophy*. Ibadan, Nigeria: University of Ibadan Press.

Soyinka, Wole. 1999. *The Burden of Memory, the Muse of Forgiveness*. Oxford: Oxford University Press.

Staniland, Hilary Susan. 2014. *Universals*. London: Palgrave.

Steven, S. O. 2011. "Cartesian Dualism: An Evaluation of Wireduan and Gilbert Ryle's Refutation." *Kritike* 5, no. 2: 156–65.

Taiwo, O. 2005. "Post-Independence African Political Philosophy." In *A Companion to African Philosophy*, edited by Kwasi Wiredu, 243–59. London: Routledge.

———. 2010. *How Colonialism Preempted Modernity in Africa*. Bloomington: Indiana University Press.

———. 2014. *Africa Must Be Modern: A Manifesto*. Bloomington: Indiana University Press.

———. 2016. "Against African Communalism." *Journal of French and Francophone Philosophy—Revue de la philosophie française et de langue française* 24, no. 1: 81–100.

Tambiah, Stanley. 1990. *Magic, Science, Religion, and the Scope of Rationality*. Cambridge: Cambridge University Press.

Tar, U. A. 2010. "The Challenges of Democracy and Democratisation in Africa and Middle-East." *Information, Society and Justice* 3, no. 2: 81–94.

Taylor, C. 1992. "The Politics of Recognition." In *Multiculturalism and the Politics of Recognition*, edited by A. Gutmann. Princeton, NJ: Princeton University Press, 25–74.

Teffo, J. 2005. "Democracy, Kingship, and Consensus: A South African Perspective." In *A Companion to African Philosophy*, edited by Kwasi Wiredu, 443–49. London: Routledge.

Thiong'o, Ngugi Wa. 1986. *Decolonising the Mind: The Politics of Language in African Literature*. Portsmouth, NH: Heinemann.

Udoidem, S. I. 1987. "Wiredu on How Not to Compare African Thought with Western Thought: A Commentary." *African Studies Review* 30, no. 1: 101–4.

Uwizeyimana, D. E. 2012. "Democracy and Pretend Democracies in Africa: Myths of African Democracies." *Law, Democracy and Development* 16:139–61.

Venter, D. 2003. "Democracy and Multiparty Politics in Africa." *EASSRR* 19, no. 1: 1–39.

Wamala, E., 2005. "Government by Consensus: An Analysis of a Traditional Form of Democracy." In *A Companion to African Philosophy*, edited by Kwasi Wiredu, 433–42. London: Routledge.

Wamba-dia-Wamba, E., and Mahmood Mamdani, eds. 1995. *African Studies in Social Movements and Democracy*. Dakar, Senegal: CODESRIA.

Weir, Alan. 2006. "Indeterminacy of Translation." In *The Oxford Handbook of Philosophy of Language*, edited by Ernest Lepore and Barry Smith, 233–50. Oxford: Oxford University Press.

Wilson, Brian, ed. 1970. *Rationality*. New York: Harper Torchbooks.

Winch, Peter. 1958. *The Idea of the Social Sciences and its Relation to Philosophy*. London: Routledge.

———. 1964. "Understanding a Primitive Society." *American Philosophical Quarterly* 1:307–24.

———. 1997. "Can We Understand Ourselves?" *Philosophical Investigations* (July): 193–204.

Wittgenstein, Ludwig. 1979. *Remarks on Frazer's Golden Bough*, edited by R. Rhees, translated by A. C. Miles and R. Rhees. Atlantic Highlands, NJ: Humanities.

———. 1980. *Culture and Value*, edited and translated by Peter Winch. Chicago: University of Chicago Press.

———. 1980. *Remarks on the Philosophy of Psychology*, vol. 1, translated by G. E. M. Anscombe. Oxford: Basil Blackwell.

Wright, Crispin, and C. Wright. 2017. "Indeterminacy of Translation." In *A Companion to the Philosophy of Language*, 670–702. Chichester, UK: John Wiley & Sons.

INDEX

BARRY HALLEN has been Reader in Philosophy, Obafemi
Awolowo University, Ile-Ife, Nigeria; Fellow and Associate of
the W. E. B. Du Bois Institute for African and African American
Research, Harvard University; and Professor of Philosophy and
Chair of the Department of Philosophy and Religion at Morehouse
College, Atlanta, Georgia. He is author of *The Good, the Bad, and
the Beautiful: Discourse about Values in Yoruba Culture* and *A Short
History of African Philosophy, Second Edition.*

Lightning Source UK Ltd.
Milton Keynes UK
UKHW011410040321
379780UK00003B/139